THE CHRISTIAN BROTHERHOOD HOUR PULPIT

Notable Sermons of
W. Dale Oldham
R. Eugene Sterner
James Earl Massey

Edited by Maurice Berquist

Published by

warnerpress
Anderson, Indiana

Contents

Introduction

Maurice Berquist
Executive Secretary, Mass Communications Board

The cold air bristled with sound. Steel struck stone as the spirited horses pawed the cobblestone streets of Rome. The shouting of a hysterical crowd was pierced by the shrill trumpets. Victory had come again.

Through the hastily constructed Victor's Arch rode the conquering army. Rome was triumphant, for Rome now ruled the world. Caesar was god, and if not the only god, he was godlike in his power.

Common people both feared and trusted this power. Certainly it filled the city with slaves, but it made them reluctantly happy that someone was in control. Even a brutal ruler was better than no ruler at all.

While the songs of victory echoed against the walls of pagan temples and the air was electric with excitement, a silent drama was unfolding. There is always a hidden drama where some quiet miracle is taking place.

In the case of the infancy of Christianity, it was drama in a dungeon. Wrapped in an ancient cloak stained with salt water shivered a lonely man. He hunched over a piece of papyrus and wrote. The feeble light filtering in through the tiny cell window and the dimness of his sight combined to make his task difficult.

Were it not for the light in his deep-set eyes and the warmth of his zeal, it would have been too dark and cold to write.

Paul, the apostle, wrote. Once more the Word of God clothed itself in flesh. The calloused hands of a tentmaker held a pen—or was it a scepter? Words quietly penned in a prison would shake the world. To the brazen boasts of the world's leaders, judgment came. The inevitable hour. The Word of God will abide forever.

One does not have to be a Christian to see the divine strategy. People are sent. Like arrows hurled from the taut bowstring, they fly to their appointed target. *Apostle* is the right word for them—they are persons sent. Paul was not the last.

Why is it surprising to us to learn that we are a part of history? Those who make up the illustrious past—the glorious yesterdays—lived every moment of their life in a time called "today." They did not think of themselves as "giants of history." They may or may not have had any awareness of the importance of their part in history. They were, however, strongly aware of their personal obedience to a divine call.

In the pages that follow you are invited to walk in the thoughtful steps of three important men in the history of the Church. They do not think of themselves as giants, but they are not asked to assess their role.

These three persons have been chosen as speakers for the Christian Brotherhood Hour, the radio voice of the Church of God (Anderson, Indiana). In this responsible office they have lifted up the major themes of the Bible and have given them pointed application to the world they live in. Each has set his unique stamp upon the message in the same way that the God-appointed authors of the first four books of the New Testament recorded many of the same events from their personal perspective.

Looking back at the messages of the first thirty-three years of the Christian Brotherhood Hour, we are impressed with two things. First, we are impressed with the depth and dimension of Scripture. "Though sin is shown to be wide and deep, thank God his grace is wider and deeper still" (Rom. 5:20, Phillips). Reading these messages that span thirty-three years of change makes one realize that it is the nature of eternal truth to be timely.

Next, we are impressed with the value of looking at the same things through different eyes. For this reason, this collection of Christian Brotherhood Hour messages will give new interest to old ideas.

It is fitting that this volume appears during the Centennial year in this church's life. Anniversaries give us an opportunity to look at changes and changelessness. If the church is thought of in terms of a "reformation movement" it emphasizes the idea that *reformation* and *evolution* are not the same thing. *Reformation* assumes that what an organization was "formed" to be, it still needs to be. *Evolution* assumes that what an organization was formed to be is no longer adequate, hence the change.

The editor has selected from each speaker's radio work messages that are both timely and timeless. They deal with pivotal and central themes rather than peripheral and passing tendencies. The biblical and doctrinal base of each sermon is clearly seen and adequately regarded.

It is always risky to label preaching as "doctrinal." Doctrine is not scaffolding. It is structure. Although the messages selected for this volume have proved appealing, judged by the number of requests for copies, their popularity was not the only reason for their inclusion. Whether they speak about God, Christ, the Holy Spirit, the Church, or the common situations and ventures of life, they are messages that live. They come from life and speak to life.

Through these thirty-three years, the Christian Brotherhood Hour has spoken of a "united Church for a divided world." While this is a specific goal of the Church of God, it is a mandate for the programming of the Christian Brotherhood Hour. No sectarian bias or narrowly local reference could find its way into the message. The Bible itself must become the means of uniting people—not dividing them.

A thoughtful reading of these messages will convince anyone that this was not only a dream, it was the normal characteristic of each presentation.

The editor has selected from each speaker's work one sermon that focuses on the hearer's personal worth, one sermon about God's ways with us, one sermon about the person of Jesus Christ, one sermon about how the Holy Spirit relates to our living, one sermon about the meaning and work of the Church, and three situational or spot sermons about how to handle life and deal with personal problems.

Three Colorful Personalities

Dr. W. Dale Oldham was the founding speaker of the Christian Brotherhood Hour. It would be easy to write that he appeared on the weekly broadcast for twenty-one years, from 1947 to 1968. That would be only part of the truth. Every broadcast from the first to the ones that are alive on the air as this is written bears the unmistakable stamp of W. Dale Oldham.

In a unique way, Dr. Oldham is able to "anchor dreams to earth with deeds."

A dreamer he was. When the idea of a national radio broadcast came into the minds of Richard Lee Meischke and Dr. Oldham, it was a vision of faith. If it should be done, it could be done. And if it could be done, it ought to be begun by those who dreamed of it.

What are the personal characteristics of this man who was to be "Mr. CBH" for millions around the world.

In the early days, the theme song for Christian Brotherhood Hour was "Rise Up O Men of God." There is something of the shrill insistance of a trumpet in that song. "If the trumpet give an uncertain sound, who shall prepare himself to the battle," says the Scripture (1 Cor. 14:8, KJV). Clarity and brilliance characterized Dr. Oldham's style. His resonant voice made even the most carefully chosen words sound better than they had any claim to sound. The driving insistence on righteousness that is the obvious life-style of Dr. Oldham became the mood of the broadcast. There was no need to introduce this man with flamboyant language; he was his own declaration.

In tribute to Dr. Oldham the Mass Communications Board of the Church of God appointed him "Speaker Emeritus" in 1977.

When it was learned that Dr. Oldham was going to retire from the active radio ministry, everyone was troubled and wondered who could step into these shoes and carry the message in the way that Dr. Oldham did.

Fortunately those who were faced with finding a replacement were wise enough to know that they did not need to find anyone to walk in Dr. Oldham's shoes; he would still be walking in them. What was needed was another person who could let God work through their lives in a very creative way. God had prepared a man.

Through years of ministry at many levels—national, international, and pastoral—Dr. R. Eugene Sterner was fully qualified to accept the responsibility.

At once there was a change. It was as though the conductor of the orchestra had silenced the trumpet section and had nodded to the woodwinds. The warm compassionate style of Dr. Sterner soon won new listeners. The integrity of the man, the thoroughness of his labor, and the intensity of his purpose all came through clearly. It is not fair to compare anyone with anyone, but to point up the strengths of both of these two remarkable men the editor will risk a comparison. Dr. Oldham was the general of the army. He blew the Trumpets and mobilized the troops. Dr. Sterner was the foot soldier who walked along beside you. Both types are needed.

When Dr. Sterner retired from the active radio ministry in 1977 he was designated "Speaker at Large."

As these words are written, there is a tendency to say that each of the three men who has carried the title, "Radio Minister of the Church of God," is unique. Of course that is true, but it is also true that everyone who breathes is unique. What is important is that each of these men is unique in significant ways.

Following the illustrious ministries of Dr. Oldham and Dr. Sterner is the ministry of Dr. James Earl Massey. Missionary, pastor, writer and college professor, Dr. Massey's scholarly gifts had found wide use in the church. As he accepted the role of speaker for the Christian Brotherhood Hour, he brought new strengths to the program. To elaborate these strengths would be

9

like giving a thumbnail sketch of the style of the Apostle Paul. It would be like playing a Beethoven concerto with one hand.

Dr. Massey is first of all a scholar of the Bible. That fact alone might make him a researcher, scarcely a "clarion call to righteousness." Scholarship is for the man a life-style, but it serves to unite him to the world of people. As the carefully chosen words reach the ears and hearts of millions of listeners, the words of scripture are being fulfilled: "Thy word is a lamp unto my feet and a light unto my path."

Brilliance is there, but it is at a place where it can do the most good. The Bible becomes "light for walking," not merely brilliance for admiring.

Dr. Massey's style is deliberate and thoughtful. If we can continue the metaphor of the orchestra, Dr. Oldham may be the trumpet section, Dr. Sterner the woodwinds, and Dr. Massey is some of all of them, but his job is to repeat the theme again and again. Sometimes it is played on the trumpets, sometimes on the flutes, and sometimes rhythms are sounded out on the percussion instruments. But whatever the particular emphasis, the message comes through: "This is what the whole Bible is all about."

W. Dale Oldham
Founding Speaker, Christian Brotherhood Hour
1947-1968

Hidden Among the Baggage

"And the Lord said, 'Behold, he has hidden himself among the baggage' " (1 Samuel 10:22, RSV).

Israel had been clamoring for a king. It wasn't that they couldn't get along without one. Wasn't the Lord God the supreme monarch of his people? Yes, but other nations had kings, and it has been the weakness of people in all ages to be discontented until they become like their neighbors. Again and again this tendency was to lead Israel into trouble. On the other hand, the elders of Israel cannot be blamed for desiring a firmer leadership for the people. Samuel had grown old and infirm, and in his declining years had appointed his sons to be judges over Israel. These younger men lacked the integrity of their father. They had used their office for personal gain, accepted bribes, perverted judgment. No wonder the people complained! But when they voiced their complaints to Samuel, he felt that their attitude constituted a rejection of his leadership. However, the Lord said, "They have not rejected you, but they have rejected *me* from being king over them" (1 Sam. 3:7). Samuel warned the people, tried to dissuade them from their purpose, but to no avail. They said, "We will have a king over us, that we also may be like all the nations, and that our king may govern us and go out before us and fight our battles" (1 Sam. 8:19-20). How naive they were! The king would not fight *their* battles, they would fight *his*.

12

So now, although Samuel had already secretly anointed Saul to be king, he set in motion a kind of lottery by which, first, the tribe of Benjamin was chosen. Then from that tribe, the family of Matri was chosen; from the family of Matri, the lot finally fell on Saul. But when they sought for him, Saul was not to be found. Anticipating this moment, he had hidden himself, probably in a wagon, among the baggage. Tall, handsome, intelligent he may have been, but at that moment he was a very frightened young man. An important job was waiting: enormous responsibilities, serious duties, a needy people were out there, expecting him to step forth and lay a firm hand on the helm of the ship of state, but Saul had run away and hidden himself. You can see him, can't you—a big fellow—head and shoulders taller than anyone else. He was handsome, good-looking, but now crouched on hands and knees behind a large box or a pile of tents in a wagon, hiding. He was hidden from Samuel, the man of God, hidden from the people who clamored to make him king, and hidden from all who needed him. Yes, he was found shortly, and brought out to face the music, but all the rest of his life he would remember how, when God's hand was laid upon him, he had run away.

Did you ever run away from duty, from the call of God? Many people are today hiding among the baggage of the twentieth century, hiding from a seeking, searching Savior, hiding from a church which needs their help. They are hiding from a hungry, lost world of people. But where does a person find fulfillment and life's true meaning? Certainly it cannot be found by hiding, by turning your back on responsibility, by shutting people out, by closing your ears to the insistent, urgent pleas of those in need. Crouching behind the baggage, Saul was more coward than king. His thoughts were far more on himself than on the needs of others. He was hoping that if he remained hidden, circumstances might change and the people might choose someone else in his place. But they found him, brought him out, and forced him to assume the title and responsibility of a king.

How many potentially great people are hidden among the baggage today! For example, the Church around the world is suffering from a serious shortage of talented, qualified, well-trained pastors. I cannot believe that this situation prevails because there are not enough gifted persons in the world to supply the need. No, the talented people are there, but they have not made themselves available to Christ and the Church. God has endowed them with wonderful talents and abilities, but they are using them for selfish purposes. Meanwhile, the Church suffers for lack of the intelligent, inspired leadership which these persons *should* be providing. Today there are many successful business and professional men and women who ought to be in the ministry, and would be in the ministry if they would listen to the call of God, if they had a consecration equal to their talents. Some are making a great deal of money, but they will come to the end of the journey with the feeling that life tricked them and that they were foolishly persuaded to sell their birthright for a mess of pottage. There are school teachers who ought to be preaching, insurance agents who ought to be presenting Christ to a lost world. If God has called you to preach the gospel, you cannot justify the sidestepping of that call by giving gifts of money to the Church. When God wants *you*, don't offer him money as a substitute.

Perhaps Saul hid because he just didn't want to be a king. Perhaps he wanted to go on with his farming, his hunting, and his fishing. Many people are ruining their lives today, through a blinding, deadening preoccupation with self. Their own little world has become more important to them than the great big world just outside their window. A year or two ago someone discovered a man living deep in the Ozark Mountains for whom the outside world simply did not exist. He had no radio, no telephone, received no newspaper. He lived alone on his little acreage and let the rest of the world go by. He did not know who was president of the United States and did not know there had been a Second World War. He knew nothing about television or the coming of the atomic age. He seemed to possess no feeling of obligation as a citizen. His was a total preoccupation with self.

You don't have to be hidden back in the mountains to be preoccupied with self. It can happen to a person surrounded by people every hour of every day. You can simply ignore the problems, troubles, needs, worries, fears, and sufferings of those about you. You can hide among the baggage and refuse to come forth to serve. You can give yourself to the pursuit of things or pleasure, even legitimate vocations or hobbies, to the exclusion of everything else and everyone else. In 1 Timothy 5:6 we read, "She that liveth in pleasure (or self-indulgence as one translation has it) is dead while she liveth" (KJV). How many people are so preoccupied with the pursuit of pleasure, so preoccupied with self-indulgence, that they are hidden to all the higher joys, satisfactions, and values of life! If you wish to hide from duty and responsibility, there is plenty of baggage to shut you from view. Never were more apparently legitimate alibis available to all of us. Demanding jobs, overtime work, family needs, houses to be painted, automobiles to be repaired, relatives to be visited—these are all legitimate things which clamor for time and attention, and if we choose to do so we can be hidden among them to the exclusion of all else, even God. But the fact is that if we take God into our work, our family relationships, and our movement through the community, then the very things which hide others from joy will actually serve as our finest sources of satisfaction and Christian pleasure.

Well, are you hidden among the baggage or facing up to life? Are you accepting the will of God for your life, or running away from the call of duty? Have you shaken off the hand of God from your shoulder? Are you reluctant to accept the adult, mature responsibilities which the nature of your talents indicates you should be undertaking? Is someone else having to carry your share of Christian responsibilities? Is someone else standing in the pulpit you should be occupying? Is someone teaching the class you should be instructing? Is someone else having to donate the money you should be giving? Is someone else straining to evangelize the people you should be garnering in for the Lord? Are you too busy—too busy to discover and follow God's will for your life? Too busy doing what? Will what you are doing justify you in the Day of judgment?

This is a distracting world in which we are living, my friend. Don't let your eyes wander from the one true goal. Don't get lost among the baggage. Don't lose God out of your life, or you will have lost all. Jesus said, "But seek ye first the kingdom of God, and his righteousness, and all these things shall be added unto you" (Matt. 6:33). Let's come out from our hiding places, assume the responsibilities God has ordained that we should carry, and we will then enjoy both day and night the satisfactions which are known only to those who give the Lord first place in their lives. God bless you.

Is God a Spy?

"If I sin, what is that to thee, O thou spy upon mankind?" (Job 7:20, Moffatt).

These modern speech versions of the Bible startle us sometimes with their frank translations This particular translation is dependable, but it sounds sacrilegious, almost blasphemous. You just don't talk to God like that! However, perhaps you can understand a man's temporary irritability when he has suffered as much as Job, when he has been forsaken by his wife, when he has lost his children and is being severely criticized by his friends. Job was speaking right out, bluntly and critically. At the moment he did not feel that God was a friend at all, but a great spy, eager to discover a reason for punishing him. He further said, "Let me alone! What is man . . . that thou should'st inspect him every morning?" Job was wanting God to look the other way for awhile.

And no wonder! Although his conscience was clear enough, his three miserable "comforters" were accusing him of secret sin, insisting that all his suffering and loss was sent by God to punish him for secret wrongdoing. They were trying to convince Job that no one suffers as he was without deserving to suffer.

But these three conversationalists were wrong—dead wrong. They knew little of the true nature of God. Jesus said that God is a loving heavenly Father, anxious to hear and answer prayer.

They said that God was eager to punish people for sin, by sending sickness, trouble, and other misfortunes upon them. I'm glad I wasn't brought up to think like that about God! I cannot imagine a loving God being vindictive or hateful, can you? But these fellows almost had Job convinced at least for awhile. He was even having nightmares about God!

Years ago I was singing in meetings with a well-known evangelist who, in spite of his fair education, was given to making grammatical errors now and then. An older preacher used to take delight in writing down these errors and later handing them to my friend. One day it was the older man's turn to preach, and as he entered the pulpit, my friend took out a notebook and pen as if in readiness to write. It so upset the speaker that he did a very poor job, and when the service was over he came quickly and asked to see the paper. It was a blank. Not a word had been written on it, but he learned his lesson. You do not like to see someone with pad and pencil waiting for you to blunder. Job didn't like the idea of God's doing this either.

Job said, "If I sin, what harm is that to thee, O thou spy upon mankind?" Job wasn't meaning to be sacrilegious or shocking. He was simply in trouble, deep trouble, and trying to silence his accusers. Also, he was ill and bereft of his family. His wealth was gone and his friends were proving untrue. Satan's pressure was on. It was a war of nerves. Some time ago a man was relating an experience he had undergone as a witness in a murder trial. An expert lawyer defended the murderer and used every skill and trick at his command. My friend was a strong young man, but was so exhausted after having undergone cross examination that he had to stretch out on a bench for some time in order to recover.

Remember, Job had suffered one reverse after another without an opportunity to recuperate in between blows. Suppose *you* had just lost your property, your home, your children, your health, the loyalty of your wife—all within a few days time. Suppose pain was wracking your body, you were broken out all over with boils, and it appeared you might never be well again. Then suppose that your three best friends would also turn against you, accusing you of a wickedness of which you were perfectly innocent. Now can you understand why Job felt like a cornered, wounded animal? Can you understand why he was irritable, even with God? Why bother to go on? Why not do as his faithless wife suggested: curse God and die. Human sympathy lends great support in time of trouble. But Job had none. How many of us might have succumbed to life's bombardments at some time or other had it not been for true friends who stood by with their love and wonderful words of encouragement. Job's miserable friends let him down when he needed them most.

However, being resentful against God never solves our problems. Indeed, it creates more problems. We'll confess, this *is* a difficult world in which to spend seventy years. For a while it must have seemed to Job that the battle was impossible, that he must lose the fight. Yet God brought him through like a conqueror. In a tremendous surge of faith he finally exclaimed, "Though he slay me, yet will I trust him" (13:15, KJV).

The Bible says that the eyes of the Lord are upon us always, beholding the evil and the good. Does this justify us in calling God, as did Job, a "spy upon mankind"? No! God *does* watch over us, but not to criticize. God watches because he loves us. God watches because he would protect us, guide us, bless us. God knows life is a struggle for us. That's why he has promised his all-sufficient grace. God knows that our hearts are sometimes broken by grief and disappointment. That's why he has promised never to leave us or forsake us. God knows how life is always bombarding us from all directions. That's why he has promised, "I will be with you in trouble."

God does look down upon us, but not as a spy. God must look with anxiety sometimes as he sees our wavering, our fear, our weakness. God wants us to live so he can bless us, help us, have fellowship with us. God wants to keep us free from the defiling elements of this world because he knows that "whatsoever a man soweth, that shall he also reap" (Gal. 6:7, KJV). He follows us for good, not for harm. Our sin is significant because it erects a barrier between us and God, but the barrier is our doing, not God's.

19

The text said, "If I sin, what harm is that to thee?" Well, our sin may not harm God, but I'm sure it saddens him because it blocks divine benevolent intentions toward us. These words were addressed to God by Job, but let everyone ask this same question of others, for one of the saddest by-products of our sin is what it does to other people. The sins of the fathers are visited upon the children to the third and fourth generation, not by the ill will of God but as a result of the laws of influence. The ungodly father brings up an ungodly son; the irreligious mother brings up an irreligious daughter. Parents can expect their children to reflect their own lack of piety and reverence. A father may ask of his son, "If I sin, what harm is that to thee?" The answer may be delayed for a few years, but it will finally come. "Like father, like son," we say, "like mother, like daughter."

Never forget, father and mother, the moral and spiritual laws of our universe never cease working. Eventually we reap the harvest of the seed we have sown, regardless of its quality, be it righteousness or sin. In Psalm 33:12 we read, "Blessed is the nation whose God is the Lord" (KJV). You could also say, "Blessed is that marriage and blessed is that family whose God is the Lord."

A husband may say to his wife by his very acts, "If I sin, what harm is that to thee?" What harm, indeed? Doesn't she have the right to expect loyalty and love from her husband? Hasn't God intended that she should be able to depend on him, draw strength and security from him? What a violation of the laws of love sin is. When sin enters a marriage, happiness flees. When a husband gives himself to sin, he can expect the former family joys to depart. When a wife gives herself to sin, she is playing squarely into the hands of Satan. Gone is peace of mind; gone is the former sense of security and well-being. Instead there is anxiety, worry, fear—a certain foreboding in facing the future. What a terrible price husbands and wives and their children pay for the questionable privilege of sinning. I once visited a family where every child was physically abnormal because of a profligate father. A young man married a lovely girl, pure and sweet. But after they had been married awhile he began to have affairs with other women. He too might have asked his wife, "If I sin, what harm is that to thee?" He wouldn't have waited long for an answer, for their first baby was born blind as a result of the father's syphilitic infection received as a direct result of his sinning.

Father, you cannot live sinfully without affecting your children. Mother, you cannot turn your back on your home and family without the children's being the chief sufferers. I hate divorce and the sinfulness and disloyalty which leads to divorce partly because of the terrible price the children must pay for their parents' sinfulness. It is the children who pay as they are brought up by their grandparents or their aunts and uncles or a stepparent to whom they are an undesirable burden.

"If I sin what harm is that to thee?" Take the text literally. If I should be taken in grievous sin, would you be affected? Yes, even if we have never met personally. Every sin anyone commits creates its own large or small circle of influence. Someone, and often a great many people, must help pay the bill. It is unfair to God, unfair to people, unfair to your family, and unfair to yourself for you to live outside of Christ. Won't you accept this fact? Then turn to our Lord in repentance and faith and save yourself and those you love from having to harvest the crop of your sinning. There is no better time to turn to the Savior than right now.

This Eternal Christ

"Jesus Christ is the same yesterday, today and forever" (Heb. 13:8, NEB).

What a person, what a personality—this Christ! Eternal in love, gracious in power, patient beyond description, he abides forever. In John 8:58 he said he was in existence before the time of Abraham. Abraham lived about nineteen hundred years before Christ. No wonder this strange Son of God defies our fullest efforts toward understanding him. He became a man, but he was from the beginning more than a man. He assumed human form, but he was and is, as the theologians put it, "very God of very God." In John 17:5 Jesus said he shared glory with our heavenly Father before the creation of the world. In verse 24 he said he was loved of the Father "before the foundation of the world" (RSV). Paul said of Jesus in Colossians 1:17, "He is before all things, and by him all things consist" (KJV). In Revelation 1:8 we have our Lord saying, "I am Alpha and Omega, the beginning and the ending . . . which *is,* and which *was,* and which is to come" (KJV).

Because Jesus is, and forever has been, co-eternal with the Father, he is the one we need every moment of life. Ponder carefully the words of our text: Jesus Christ, the same yesterday. . . ." I find little happiness in thinking about my yesterdays, and in this, I am sure, many of you would join me.

Those yesterdays were days of sin, days of rebellion against the will of God, days when we rejected his saving grace and pardoning love. Yet it was in one of those yesterdays that he finally won my heart, forgave my sins, healed my life. I was *so* miserable! When you know what is right, but refuse to do it, when you know the way but aren't walking in it, when a divine invitation is extended to you and you are not accepting it, you are, by the very nature of things, a miserable and unhappy person. I was! Then this eternally-the-same Christ offered full forgiveness, merciful peace, conquering power in the giving of himself for the needs of my soul. I accepted and have never for a moment regretted it. My past is gone, adequately taken care of by the love of Christ. It has lost all of its former power to condemn me, to weigh me down with a burden of guilt. As Paul wrote in Romans 8:1 2, ''There is therefore now no condemnation to them which are in Christ Jesus, who walk not after the flesh, but after the Spirit. For the law of the Spirit of life in Christ Jesus hath made me free from the law of sin and death'' (KJV).

No one but Christ could do this for me, but he did it. My life was completely changed by his transforming love and power. Thank God for the power exercised by Christ *yesterday*. It was yesterday that he also forgave Mary Magdalene and Peter, the inconsistent, wavering one. It was yesterday that he forgave a woman guilty of serious sin, healed a man who had been born blind, restored honesty and self-respect to Zacchaeus, a hated collector of taxes. Yesterday Christ had power and used it, not for selfish purposes, but for the blessing of humanity.

But that was yesterday. What about today? Well, as the song has it,

Yes, he healed in Galilee,
Set the suff'ring captives free,
And he's just the same today.

Thank God! He *is* just the same today—still in the saving business, still in the healing business, still working miracles whereby self-respect is restored and new courage given. As God dealt with my past, so God supports me in the present. It is wonderful that God came to redeem my life from destruction years ago, but my gratitude is just as great for what God is doing for me *now*. An elderly brother used to rise in testimony meeting to say, "Praise God! Jesus saves me *now*!" To which many of us would like to add a hearty and grateful "Amen!" Our Lord is not an antiquated Christ but a present Savior, a friend who abides.

You have no doubt sung the song which says,

> And he walks with me,
> And he talks with me
> And he tells me I am his own.[1]

We need that kind of a Christ to help us face *today's* needs, *today's* troubles and trials, *today's* threats of personal or world disaster. Thank God! Jesus Christ *is* the same yesterday and today! I want him today! I need him today! I have him today! If, in this twentieth century, the world blunders on without the leadership of Christ, it is not because that guidance is unavailable. If people persist in continuing in their evil ways of living, it is not because deliverance is beyond their reach. A present Christ is offered to every needy heart. A forgiving Christ stands ready to lift burdens of condemnation from repentant souls. This Christ can save *today* as surely as he redeemed men and women from sin nineteen centuries ago. His encouraging, supporting power is denied none who come to him with broken and contrite hearts.

How desperately people need Christ today! Yet many seem totally unaware of what he could do for them. Marriages that are failing could be turned toward success if husband and wife would submit their hearts to Christ. Reconciliation would come, not through arbitration, but through a changing of their hearts. Many marriages fail through sheer selfishness, unwillingness to share, or the inability of one or the other to turn away from a devastating preoccupation with self. Remember, there is no adequate substitute for the grace of God. There is no workable counterfeit for divine love. It takes the real thing—genuine conversion—to re-center our lives and give new direction to our motives. But a present Christ can and will do this for all who honestly and earnestly come to him for aid.

24

"Jesus Christ is the same yesterday, today, and forever." What he was in the past, he is now and forever will be. He never changes. His mercy is from everlasting to everlasting. His compassion knows no limit. His ability and desire to forgive are never diminished, and never will be. Who knows what will happen tomorrow? No one. Who can say what will be the condition of the world in a year or ten years? No one. But this we do know: When tomorrow comes, Christ will be there. When a new day dawns, it will reveal his continuing glory. As the years roll by, time will but ratify the fact that Christ's love never fails, and his mercy is undiminished. Thank God!

> Many things about tomorrow
> I don't seem to understand;
> But I know who holds tomorrow,
> And I know who holds my hand.[2]

The years are rapidly advancing. Every hour hastens for each of us the end of life. Before long we must walk out into the sunset to discover first hand what eternity is like. Are you afraid of the crossing? Is there any reason for anxiety as you await the call? Will the eternal Christ fail us as we step into the river of death? Never! Never! Not if our trust is in him. Not if we have walked in humble, loving obedience before him. The Christ who wrought salvation within our hearts yesterday, who keeps us, loves us, guides and comforts us today, will not change when tomorrow dawns. Forever he is the same! What he promised his disciples is promised to us. He said, "I will not leave you comfortless" (John 14:18, KJV). And again, "I will never leave thee, nor forsake thee" (Heb. 13:5).

Faith is a basic need of the human heart, and it is with Christian faith that we face the unknown future. God is our keeper; Christ is our friend. As David said in Psalm 27:1, "The Lord is my light and my salvation; whom shall I fear? The Lord is the strength of my life; of whom shall I be afraid?" (KJV) God will not change. What God has promised, God will do. Christ will not change. He is utterly dependable. He will stand by us staunchly, in death and beyond the grave. May our confidence in him never waver.

25

Mark Rutherford tells of a watchmaker of unusual skill and accuracy who, while crossing a sandbar at low tide one hot afternoon, lay down to rest for a moment on the sand beside a great rock, only to awaken later surrounded by the rising tide. There was no way of escape. He knew that high tide would come at 8:57 P.M. It was now 7:30. He calculated that if his watch was dependable, the tide would not quite reach his lips at the rate it was rising. But if his watch was faulty, he would be drowned. It was a good time piece and he had every reason to trust it, but as the water slowly rose, terrible fears assailed him. However, faith won the battle. Listen! "The flutter of his heart ceased; the adversary spread his wings and was seen no more." At 8:50 the tide reached his neck, but he just lifted his head a bit higher, confident that the moment of deliverance was at hand. At 8:58 the waters halted and ultimately subsided. The watchmaker's confidence in his time piece was vindicated. Well, our trust in *Christ* will be vindicated also! He who holds in his hands the secret of immortality will not fail us when the waters rise about us. He who is "the same yesterday, today, and forever" will be there to lift us up and out and to guide us safely home. Trust in his mercy, rest in his grace, walk obediently before him, and all will be well, now and throughout the ceaseless ages of eternity.

Have You Received the Holy Spirit?

"Have ye received the Holy Ghost since ye believed?" (Acts 19:2, KJV).

The Day of Pentecost has well been called "the birthday of the Church," for on that day the Holy Spirit came upon the group of 120 Christian believers assembled in an upper room in Jerusalem, bestowing upon them a new fragrance, power, effectiveness, courage, and daring. For us today to ignore what happened at Pentecost would be like ignoring the discovery of electricity and its use.

Every mature Christian can remember at least three stages of spiritual development. The first stage was those years of being the victim of sin. Bound by chains of evil habit, a sense of guilt never left. It was a time of being fully aware of deserving the wrath of God, the condemnation and judgments of God. Sometimes he thought the condition hopeless, and cried out with Paul, "O wretched man that I am! Who shall deliver me from the body of this death?" (Rom. 7:24). But reading Matthew 18:11, hope sprang up. Listen! "For the son of man is come to seek and to save that which was lost." Thank God! The lost can be found!

Being found of Christ represents the second stage in one's spiritual development. As we repent of our sins and believe on Christ for salvation, we are lifted out of guilt and condemnation

27

into the forgiveness of God. Paul said it like this in Romans 5:1: "Therefore, being justified by faith, we have peace with God through our Lord Jesus Christ." This is salvation—the new birth, regeneration, an experience in which old things pass away and everything becomes new. This experience was enjoyed by the disciples before the Day of Pentecost after they had forsaken all to follow Jesus.

The third stage in our Christian development is represented by Pentecost: the receiving of the Holy Spirit. Remember that the 120 assembled in the Upper Room were all Christians. They were already followers of Christ and had already experienced the forgiveness of sin. Note also the sequence of events in Acts 19:1-7. Paul found certain disciples at Ephesus. Underscore the fact that they were already disciples, and yet according to verse two they had not even heard of the Holy Spirit. Verse 5 tells us that Paul then baptized them in water which symbolically represented their death to sin. Going under the water symbolized being buried with Christ. Coming up out of the water symbolized their resurrection to new life in Christ. All this happened before verse 6, which says, "And when Paul had laid his hands upon them, the Holy Ghost came on them." This marked the beginning of the third stage of their spiritual development, as they gave themselves to God in full surrender of their redeemed bodies, souls, minds, and talents. This gave entrance into the "grace wherein we stand," referred to by Paul in Romans 5:2.

The Holy Spirit is a sanctifying power, bringing strength to the Christian, purifying motives and desires, inspiring to noble living, guiding into the ways of truth, supplying with fortitude and courage in the face of persecution, disaster, or bereavement. I like Carl Poe's story of the good, but unlearned man who had spent his life in desert country and had never seen a creek or river. Then one day, after he had boldly set out to see the world, he came to a river with a mill on its bank. Inside the mill, the maze of whirling wheels, belts, and shafts was confusing. The traveler, who had never seen machinery, stood wondering about the purpose of the various wheels and belts. Then happening to glance out a window, he saw an enormous wheel turning, agitating the water into violent motion. It dawned upon him that the machinery inside the mill was for the purpose of turning the big wheel outside and the big wheel was causing the river to flow. About that time a floating branch became entangled in the water wheel, slowing its motion, and of course, all the machinery inside slowed with it. The man felt compelled to do something about it, thinking that if the great wheel stopped the river would cease to flow. In his excitement he grabbed a belt and began to pull on it lustily, and was rewarded to see the wheels continue to turn and the river continue to flow. The conscientious fellow kept on and on at his task until at last he died, sure in the knowledge that largely through his faithful efforts the river's flow had continued. Never once did he realize it was the river which kept the machinery going, not the machinery which caused the water to flow. Today thousands of Christians struggle to maintain a spiritual vitality which they ought to realize is given freely and in power when the heart is opened wide to receive the Holy Spirit.

Have you received the Holy Spirit since you became a Christian? Why should you? What is the purpose? First, the purpose of the Spirit is to give the Christian power. Jesus said in Acts 1:8, "Ye shall receive power, after that the Holy Ghost is come upon you"—power to give an effective Christian witness. We have too many tongue-tied Christians today. They are Christians who, because they have never received the Holy Spirit, are afraid of what would be said about them if they should witness for Christ.

The power of the Holy Spirit is also the power to bear Christian fruit. The fig tree which was blighted by a word from the Master was a fruit tree all right, but it bore no fruit. There are many people who claim to be Christians, but they bear no fruit for Christ. Do they also merit his stern disapproval? In Matthew 7:20 Jesus said, "By their fruits ye shall know them." But what of the Christian who bears no fruit? This very fruitlessness reveals one's lack of power, spiritual life, and vitality. The "fruit" is seen not only in witnessing, but in attitudes, spirit, and conduct. It is seen in the quality of one's ambitions, in one's choice of friends, and in the spending of money.

The Holy Spirit gives power for genuine Christian living, and power to control our desires, our minds, our bodies. The Holy Spirit's coming provides power to love with the love of God. The Holy Spirit cancels selfishness, roots out the domineering, possessive disposition. The Holy Spirit also provides spiritual growth by bestowing certain gifts of the Spirit upon us. The right and proper use of these gifts strengthens the Church and makes its ministry more effective. The Holy Spirit gives overcoming power in the face of temptation, provides an enduring optimism to support life in the face of impending world disaster, fills the heart with faith when times are at their worst.

The Holy Spirit also guides the Christian into the ways of truth, helping to avoid serious error. In John 16:13 Jesus said, "When he, the Spirit of truth, is come, he will guide you into all truth." It is only as we live in the spirit of truth that we are guided into further truth. Christian revelation is a developing, ongoing process. Jesus knew a great many things which he could not share with his disciples, simply because they were not ready for them. How many Christians there are who cannot stand the whole truth. In 1 Corinthians 3:1-2 Paul said, "And I, brethren, could not speak unto you as unto spiritual, but as unto carnal, even as unto babes in Christ. I have fed you with milk, and not with meat: for hitherto ye were not able to bear it, neither yet now are ye able." Any church or Christian remains weak when that church or Christian is not spiritually mature enough to understand and accept the truth—the whole truth. The Spirit-filled Christian will always accept the truth and pattern life by it. The Christian whose ideas and attitudes have not changed in twenty years has stagnated. The guiding Spirit of God leads to growth, perception, development, enlargement of the soul. The person so-guided moves into a position where judgment is adult and mature, where doctrinal beliefs and way of life are in full agreement. The Spirit-filled Christian is constantly asking, "What would Jesus do in a situation like this?" Stewardship of life and possessions reflect the full control of the Holy Spirit.

Have you received the Holy Spirit since you believed? How will you know? The Spirit-filled person will be conscious of a new spiritual energy, a fresh flow of inspiration, an uplift of spirit, an increase in love, a strengthening of faith, a new and continuing desire to win others to Christ. The Spirit-filled person will find surprising delight in increasing personal gifts for the support of Christian work. Tithing will no longer be painful, but will actually bring joy and a feeling of real partnership with Christ.

The Holy Spirit will also fit you into the Church. You will experience a new sense of belonging to the body of Christ, know a new delight in standing shoulder to shoulder with others in fighting the good fight of faith. Your desire for the things of the world will drop away increasingly as you draw closer and closer to God.

Again let me ask, "Have you received the Holy Spirit since you believed?" Keith Huttenlocker asks, in a sermon on the Holy Spirit, "What must a rain barrel do in order to be filled with rain?" He answers, "First it must be emptied of all other contents. Second, it must be opened toward the sky." Christian, if you would receive the Holy Spirit, be emptied of self. Then open your heart wide and fully to God and to whatever may be the divine purposes for your life.

How Christians Are One

"That they all may be one" (John 17:21, KJV).

Many serious thinkers in the Church are deeply disturbed today over the divided condition of Christendom. To add to the problem, thousands of preachers and other Christian leaders actually defend division, saying that a divided Church is more effective in its thrust and outreach. All of this seems to hide from the searching soul the true nature of the New Testament church.

Today it seems extremely hard for some people to see the Church because of the churches, to know the real because of its imitators. We need to be reminded that denominationalism, as it exists today, is a fairly modern invention. All of the denominations have come into existence during the last four and a half centuries. The history of denominationalism makes interesting reading, but many of us find it hard to believe that a system which progressively and increasingly divided Christian people, did so invariably in the will or under the guidance of God. Jesus did not pray that we should be divided for effectiveness. His prayer was that we all might be united in heart and be one in spirit.

To me the divided condition of Christianity during these past few centuries constitutes one of the scandals of history. Paul wrote to the Corinthian church, "Now I beseech you, brethren, by the name of our Lord Jesus Christ, that ye all speak the same thing, and that there be no divisions among you; but that ye be perfectly joined together in the same mind and in the same judgment'' (1 Cor. 1:10). He went on to mention the clannish, partisan strife which was splitting the church into segments. In 1 Corinthians 3:3 he wrote, "For whereas there is among you envying, and strife, and *divisions,* are ye not carnal, and walk as men?" And in Romans 16:17-18 he added, "Now I beseech you, brethren, mark them which cause divisions and offences contrary to the doctrine which ye have learned; and avoid them. For they that are such serve not our Lord Jesus Christ . . . but . . . by good words and fair speeches deceive the hearts of the simple."

You might have thought that in Corinth, Paul would have been flattered that one faction of the church had grouped itself around him. But another group found Apollos as their nucleus while still another said, "We stand with Peter." How Satan must delight in such confusion. The dividedness, of course, is not as deplorable as the bad spirit which produced it. It is this pitting of one against another which is so unchristian. It is rivalry: this insistence that you are Christian and another is not, that you hold to the faith but the other person is a heretic. And all the while he is saying the same thing about you. It is the little foxes that spoil the vines, and it is the difference in spirit, more than differences in theology, which still divide the Church.

Children of God ought to possess the spirit of God, and if they do possess that loving spirit, they will be in cooperation instead of competition with each other. The spirit of Christ is the spirit of love, and there is no envy, no boasting, no rudeness in love. The truth is, it is extremely hard to justify division in the Church because, generally speaking, division is the result of carnality. Division among Christians is both wrong and sinful. It cannot be justified in the sight of Christ or under the spirit of the gospel. How wonderful it would be if all denominational tags could be dropped and all of us would be satisfied to say, "I'm a Christian." Our present competitive system must be totally obnoxious to him who prayed that his followers might all be one.

However, there seems to be an inner spirit of unity built into the very soul of every Holy Spirit-filled Christian. This has persisted all through Christian history in asserting itself at every opportunity. John Short writes, "With what mighty impact the gospel of reconciliation could smite the evil things that bedevil mankind if all the members of the Christian church could find grace sufficient to sit down at the same table and sing the same songs, having mended the rents made in the seamless robe by the divisions and schisms and denominationalism of Christian believers!" (Interpreter's Bible, Vol. 10, p. 24). To all of this most of us would add a hearty amen. In these enlightened days it seems totally inconsistent with the spirit of Christ for two hundred or three hundred denominations to exist in his name and claim to operate, some of them exclusively, under his banner. Don't you think so?

However, popular misconceptions as to the fundamental nature of the Church continue to separate Christians today. For example, the Bible teaches that the only way you can become a member of the New Testament Church is by being "born again." By being converted, we become members of the body of Christ, which is the Church. The Lord adds us to the Church, *his* Church! In Acts 2:47 we read, "And the Lord added to the church daily such as should be (or were being) saved." Where did we get the idea that you can "join" the Church? There is no account in the New Testament of people "joining" the Church. You can't join the Church which Christ built; you can enter only through a spiritual rebirth. Now, I have no quarrel with ecclesiastics who take members into their denominations, but I do object when they make membership in a denomination synonymous with membership in the New Testament Church. These two are not the same at all, and we need to make and keep that point clear. It might be possible to join and maintain membership in certain denominations without ever being born of the Spirit, but you cannot be a member of the body of Christ, the New Testament Church, without being converted and regenerated.

Now you begin to see why the subject of Christian unity is so baffling to so many people. The only true basis for Christian unity is in Christian experience. Joining a denominational church does not necessarily prepare one for fellowship with the Church Jesus built. You don't join the body of Christ as a person joins a lodge or a luncheon club. Membership in the New Testament Church calls for one's spiritual transformation. The doctrine of Christian unity is predicated upon just such an experience. The unconverted person, even though a member of a denomination, has never been placed in the body of Christ and so how can unity with the true Church be experienced? This is why some of us are insisting that the uniting of denominations, although working toward union, leaves a great deal to be desired so far as any basic spiritual unity is concerned.

Christian unity calls for personal Christlikeness and a certain holiness of life. Sin separates people but a genuine experience in Christ will unite them, and this will be done entirely without legislative action or group decision. Christian unity is a product of the Spirit of God, moving in the hearts of *real* Christians. In our day there is a move to unite denominations, but is this Christian unity or only denominational union? Is the ecumenical movement an answer to Christ's prayer? If half the members of the denominational churches have never been born again of the Spirit, how can the uniting of such organizations constitute Christian unity? Christian unity cannot be organized, legislated, or contrived. It is experienced only by and between born-again Christians. The unity is among the sheep of Christ's fold, not the goats. It is a unity of the saints, not a unity between saints and sinners. It is a unity of the bloodwashed followers of Christ, not those who have joined a church.

In our times there has been a lamentable apostasy in Protestantism. False doctrines abound. Modernism and a life-sapping liberalism have made their destructive inroads, and as a result, many people are confused. A woman wrote recently to ask why the Christian Brotherhood Hour uses the slogan, "A united Church for a divided world." She said, "Are you trying to unite born-again Christians with church members who don't even believe in the new birth, who reject the divinity of Christ, the holy inspiration of the scriptures, holiness, the second coming of Christ, his unique sonship?" The answer of course is no. We are not joining or promoting ecumenical movements as such. But we *are* saying that converted Christians are basically one in Christ and ought to act like it. We are interested in that unity which is the result of spiritual experience, not in ecclesiastical unions as such.

But there will be little spiritual unity without personal purity, without heartfelt commitment to Christ, for what fellowship can there be between believers and unbelievers, the committed and the undedicated, saints and sinners, those of the faith and heretics? As oil and water will not mix, just so you cannot produce unity between those who really know Christ and those who know only about him.

The Church is *the Church*—not the churches—and even if you could persuade all the denominations to unite, you still would not have the kind of unity and oneness for which Christ prayed. May the Lord open our minds and hearts to this blessed truth, and may we, by our transformed lives and Christian spirit make possible the answering of Christ's prayer for the unity of all those who are saved by grace. Amen!

Come As You Are

"Come . . . without money and without price" (Isa. 55:1, KJV).

It was time for the evening meal and because we had been traveling all day, we were alert for a suitable restaurant. Finally, there it was, out at the edge of the city, with adequate parking space for the automobile. However, we hesitated a bit to enter since we were in traveling clothes. Then someone pointed to a sign which read, "Come as you are." Without further need for self-consciousness, we entered and thoroughly enjoyed a good meal.

But the sign stayed with me—"Come as you are." And I recalled the invitation extended in Revelation 22:17: "The Spirit and the bride say, come, and let him that heareth say, come. And let him that is athirst come. And whosoever will, let him take the water of life freely." What a wonderful invitation this is!

Everyone needs to feel related to God, and yet who feels worthy to stand in God's holy presence? We all hunger for peace and love, and yet, unworthy as we are, we hesitate to approach God's holy throne of grace. We feel as did Isaiah in the temple when he cried, "Woe is me! for I am undone; because I am a man of unclean lips, and I dwell in the midst of a people of unclean lips" (Isa. 6:5). But with the revelation of

37

his need came also a vision of what he could become. The last part of verse 5 of Isaiah 6 reads, "Mine eyes have seen the King, the Lord of hosts." Then the Lord said, "Thine iniquity is taken away, and thy sin purged."

When we come humbly to the Lord, just as we are, pleading his wonderful love, mercy, and grace, God forgives our sins, transforms our nature, and makes all things new. This is what I did. Living in rebellion against the Lord, how condemned was my heart! And oh, the unhappiness! But when I repented of my rebellious and sinful ways forgiveness came and a great peace flooded my soul. I came, as Isaiah said, "Without money and without price," and he gave to me the "pearl of great price." I came just as I was, clothed in the rags of unrighteousness, but God cleansed me and placed the robe of divine righteousness about my shoulders.

Are you longing for fellowship with God, but hesitating to approach the throne because of a feeling of unworthiness? Hesitate no longer. Come just as you are, for God loves you and is even now extending his sceptre of mercy toward you. Come just as you are, pleading God's love, remembering Calvary.

Remember Simon Peter, that brash, impulsive fisherman to whom Jesus said, "Follow me." What did Peter have to offer the Son of God? Unlearned, uncouth, untrained, with the smell of fish and the salt of the sea on his hands and garments, he nevertheless came to the Master just as he was and in the process was transformed by divine power. Then there was Matthew, the hated tax collector for Rome. If Rome demanded a dollar, Matthew could collect two and pocket the second, in spite of the protests of the people. Matthew's conscience may have been as heavy with guilt as that of Zacchaeus, but he came to the Savior just as he was. Our Lord forgave his sins and accepted him into full discipleship.

You too can come just as you are, for Christ Jesus came into the world to forgive and save sinners. Remember Mary Magdalene: sinful, opposed to righteousness, given to wickedness. How could such a guilty person find peace? Yet Mary came to Jesus just as she was, and this great Son of God—he who is "the same yesterday, and today and forever"—touched her with his mighty, forgiving power, cast out the evil, purified her heart, and made her fit for citizenship in the kingdom of God.

In one of her "Unshackled" radio scripts, Eugenia Price told the moving story of the conversion of Ben Engstrom. Ben had drifted from one job to another, finally playing semiprofessional baseball for a living. But nothing satisfied him. There was a restlessness he could not overcome. He liked the crowds, the celebrations of victory in the taverns, the old "wine, women and song" routine. But nothing really satisfied Ben Engstrom. He went into show business, traveled the circuits with a theatrical group until his wife told him to quit traveling and quit drinking or she would leave him. So he settled down in a steel mill town, got a job, and before long obtained an even better one. Then one day the boss said, "You're drinking on the job, Ben. This is the only warning you will get." He straightened up briefly then began drinking again, and before long lost the job he had held for twenty-nine years. Two marriages had also failed. Ben hit bottom. Soon he was on Chicago's Skid Row, washing dishes in a cheap nightclub. Then he was in the hospital and a doctor was saying, "You'll have to be placed in an institution." With a dime the doctor lent him, Ben Engstrom rode a streetcar to the Pacific Garden Mission. Bleary-eyed from drink and lack of food, his clothes soiled and dirty, unshaven and unkempt, he was down and nearly out. Then at the invitation of Harry Saulnier, mission superintendent, Ben Engstrom came to Jesus Christ. He came just as he was, got down on his knees and found forgiveness for his sins. In that very hour his life was changed, turned around, made new. And that which happened to Ben Engstrom can happen to you. *You* can come humbly to Christ, just as you are, pleading his mercy and saving grace. You can find forgiveness and the peace of God. Why don't you do it?

But Christians have a need to come to God just as they are, too. The days of spiritual need do not end with conversion. In fact, conversion is an end only to the old life of sin. Really, it is more a time of beginning, a time of spiritual adventuring, a time of conquest and victory. But it is also a time of searching and self-examination, and sometimes Christians experience periods of perplexity and temporary confusion. To be a Christian doesn't mean that all of your problems have been solved forever, nor does it mean that you have found a song which can never be interrupted. Life being what it is, many Christians find the road to spiritual growth made difficult by ancient ruts of their own making. Christians are not angels. They may indeed be very weak human beings, subject to blundering and failure. What does a blundering Christian do to improve spiritual condition? What does a failing Christian do to find more solid ground? Well, the invitation extended to the sinner is offered also to the spiritually-needy Christian: "Come just as you are."

It is wonderful to realize that God loves us in spite of all he knows about us. God loves even the stumbling children—those who are still learning to walk, those who are still in the process of learning how to live the Christian life. God loves even those who have tried and failed and are hesitant to try again. Christians do fail sometimes. Peter did. But he didn't quit. He didn't run away from God or say he would never try again. Instead, he repented, profited by his blundering, took a new grip on the promises of God, forgave himself for being so weak and cowardly, and went on to new life, new strength, and new victories in Christ. What a great Christian he became in the days which followed!

To be a Christian doesn't necessarily mean that you will never again have to say "I'm sorry" to God or to people. Christians, being human, are still subject to mistakes and blunderings. It is good for us as Christians to know that God invites *us* to approach the throne, too, just as we are, for whatever our needs may be. As the sinner needs to confess sins, just so the Christian needs to confess faults, if he or she would "grow in grace and in the knowledge of our Lord and Savior Jesus Christ" (2 Pet. 3:18).

Remember this, my friend, no matter who you are or what your condition may be, the door to God is always open to the humble soul. David said "A broken and a contrite heart, O God, thou wilt not despise (Ps. 51:17). The broken and contrite heart may belong to an unconverted sinner or to a Christian who has been overtaken by ill-considered and foolish conduct. God loves both, and invites them to come just as they are.

The father of the prodigal son seemed to completely understand his wayward boy. How full and complete was his forgiveness and his willingness to forget the past. But the prodigal had to come back home just as he was. Why don't you do this, and come back to God just as you are. No alibis, no excuses, no explanations are needed. God understands and loves you in spite of everything. God will forgive you if you ask, and will reinstate you in divine favor. The door is wide open for your return. Come on back home, won't you? Come just as you are.

So You Can't Take It Any Longer!

"For Demas hath forsaken me, having loved this present world, and is departed unto Thessalonica" (2 Tim. 4:10, KJV).

Demas had had it. He was fed up and finished! He had stood all he intended to stand and had taken all he intended to take. The bubble had burst, and in his disillusionment Demas was leaving, heading for Thessalonica and the marts of trade. However, before criticizing him too strongly, let us examine certain points in his favor, for certainly there *were* points in his favor. First, he had become a Christian at a time when Christianity was little known and very unpopular. There is little doubt that Demas was a bright, personable, intelligent young man. Would Paul have chosen any other kind? Demas had answered the call to Christian service; perhaps travel had especially appealed to him. Or it is possible he wished to escape from the domination of his father or mother or from the designs of some marriageable young female. Anyhow, give him credit for having the courage to break with the comfort and security of his home and community to launch out into a very uncertain future with an itinerant evangelist who was backed by no reliable organization and who seemed to be living a rather hand-to-mouth existence from day to day. Yes, give Demas *some* credit. He *had* gone; he *had* served; he had shared the hostility, misunderstanding, and persecution with Paul; he had shared also the poor lodgings and food, the poverty, the uncertainty with regard to what the morrow would bring. How long he held out no one can say for sure, but probably for a few years. If he had been seeking financial security, he had not found it. The future seemed to hold no hope. To Demas, all must have seemed lost. Paul was *the* Christian leader in his part of the world in those days, and Paul was in prison, soon to die. Why remain yoked up with a condemned man? With Paul imprisoned and unable to preach, income must also have been cut off or at least radically diminished. Demas may have found himself completely without funds. What was he to do? How was he to live? How would expenses be met?

Also, his was the kind of situation which lends itself to homesickness. No doubt he felt the need for the supporting strength of friendship, for the relaxed comfort of the family fireside from which he had been so long absent. Again, Demas was following a precedent set by others. Crescens had gone to Galatia; Titus had departed for Dalmatia. Only Luke remained with Paul, but he was a doctor and his personal services were needed. So, thought Demas, why carry on? Why be different? Why keep on fighting the good fight of faith?

Well, unfortunately for him and for history, he did not keep on. He couldn't "take it." The constant grind of life finally defeated him. No one enjoys persecution unless he or she is either a mental case or a *real* Christian suffering for Christ's sake. Demas had had enough persecution! He wanted to get over on the other side of the fence for awhile, move out of the focused hostility found in the limelight. He was weary of the feeling of not getting anywhere, not being wanted, not being one with the majority. He was tired of being broke all the time. He wanted to hear the pleasant clinking of gold and silver in his purse and experience again the satisfaction of buying goods and services without having the restraints of poverty curtailing him. Like the prodigal, he probably longed for lights, for youthful companionship and activity, for brisk and witty conversation. It isn't hard to understand how the world pulled on Demas. The more he thought of it, the stronger the pull became, until at last he succumbed, gave up, quit fighting, and took the easy way of non-resistance.

That is history, but it is also today's headlines, for Demas still lives in the experience of thousands of people who have lost heart, have given up, and are drifting. The great battles of life are in the heart, not outside. To maintain faith and courage, to hold on to hope, to believe when others doubt and are trying to convince you of the foolishness of faith—this is the battle. No one can win the fight without keeping focused on Christ, "the author and finisher of our faith."

The Church cannot save us, no matter how glorious its history, no matter how extended its membership. In fact, isn't it sometimes church people who give us greatest cause for discouragement? It is easy to forget the *saints* in the church as we center our gaze on the hypocrites who, without commission or permission catch up a banner and join the parade of the holy ones. It is easy to say, "This is the Church," when what we are fastening our eyes upon with hypnotic distaste is not the Church at all, but imposters claiming Christ's name while remaining strangers to his spirit. Christ reminded us that many will say, "Lord! Lord!" in the last day, only to have him reply, "I never knew you."

Of course it is difficult to hold up under certain circumstances. You can look at the weaknesses of people until you forget the strength and holding power of the everlasting arms. You can look at the hypocrite until that one assumes the threatening size and proportions of a Goliath. You can focus on the inconsistencies of others until you yourself become weak and inconsistent. You can look at the discouragement of a disturbed and vocal minority until the very heart goes out of you. You can think of how little others are giving to support the work of God, until you are too discouraged to keep up your own generous giving. Watch out, Christian! You are on dangerous territory. Discouragement is a road leading back to Thessalonica. Discouraged Christians are generally rather useless servants of God.

So you think you can't take it any longer? Can't you? What is your real trouble? Your real trouble isn't "hypocrites in the church" but a lack somewhere in your own heart and experience. Your real trouble isn't poverty, but a need for a

44

greater faith in God. Your real trouble isn't financial, but spiritual. Your real trouble doesn't center in other people, but in yourself. No one is dependent upon other persons for standing before God. There is no need for the acts or omissions of others to affect in any way your personal relationship to the Eternal.

So you can't take it any longer? Can't take the sickness! Can't take the reputation of your local congregation! Can't take the preacher and the sermons! Can't take his wife's personality! Can't take what you have referred to as "the brainless legislation of that board of trustees"! Can't take the choir, the soloist, the organist, the Sunday school teacher or superintendent! But friend, just *who* are you serving? To whom do you really belong? Under what commission do you go forward? Who is your captain? Where is your loyalty centered? Are you leaning on people or on God? Are you depending on newspaper headlines or upon the great God of creation?

Do you remember the parable of the sower, told by Jesus and recorded in Matthew 13? He said, "Some (seeds) fell upon stony places, where they had not much earth: and forthwith they sprung up, because they had no deepness of earth: and when the sun was up, they were scorched, and because they had no root, they withered away" (vv. 5-6). You see, these *seeds* couldn't take it any longer either. But why? Because the soil wasn't right. Too many stones and too little depth of earth. How easy to blame the seed, but the fault was elsewhere. How easy to blame others for our predicament when the fault is in our own hearts, our own lack of love, our own carelessness in prayer, our own neglect of the Bible, our own failure to live close to God. Had Demas possessed a greater love, he would never have left Paul to his loneliness and discomfort. He would have stood with him to the end.

There are people today who serve Christ for the loaves and fishes and depart when these are not forthcoming. Are you and I like that? What is the basis for our loyalty? Are we, like Judas Iscariot, too much concerned with the clink of money and too little concerned with human values? So you can't take it any longer! Yes, you can! Daniel did! So did the three Hebrew children! So did Paul and millions of others who were sent to their deaths true to the faith—men like the missionary, Dr. Paul Carlson, who could have escaped, but stayed on at his tasks only to be executed by enemies of freedom and truth.

You *can* take it by the grace of God! You *can* take the poverty if you must! You *can* take the misunderstanding! You *can* take the persecution! You *can* take the hardship! Paul said, "I can do *all* things through Christ which strengtheneth me" (Phil. 4:13). So can you, my friend, but you need the grace of God, the love of God, the courage and strength of our Lord Jesus Christ planted solidly in your heart. As was said to the Children of Israel long ago, "If God be God, follow him." "Choose you this day whom ye will serve." "As for me and my house, we will serve the Lord."

Don't look for *me* in Thessalonica, and I will not expect to find you there. I am going to expect you to be true at any cost, to be faithful to Christ to the end of the journey. You *can* take it! The Lord is saying to all, "My grace is sufficient for thee." You *can* take the trouble at work; you can take the trouble at home; you can take the inconsistent behavior of people. You can take anything life throws at you, for you are standing, not in your own strength but in the power of a mighty God who has promised never to leave or forsake you. So take a fresh hold on the promises of God, my Christian friend, and hold on. Our God is a great God who will never fail you. Hold on, I say. Dare to be true, and you will have your reward in heaven.

What to Do with Your Anxieties

"Don't worry at all then about tomorrow. Tomorrow can worry about itself" (Matt. 6:34, Phillips).

How easy it is to advise everyone not to worry. How casually we say, "Don't worry. Everything will come out all right." But this is a tough world in which we are living and there is a great deal of unfriendliness and tragedy in it. Everything simply doesn't come out all right for everyone. The Bible says, "We know that in everything God works for good with those who love him, who are called according to his purpose" (Rom. 8:28, RSV). But who can fail to be somewhat affected at least by irresponsible conduct on the part of our neighbors, our friends, our relatives? Who can watch a dissolute person throw life away and not be deeply concerned about it? Who can watch a teen-ager mortgage the future with ungodliness and not be distressed? This is a world of trouble. It is the kind of trouble which doesn't disappear simply by ignoring it. When you see any person recklessly throwing away virtue, morality, honesty, decency, and an adult sense of responsibility, of course you will be concerned. How could you close your eyes to the lost in your neighborhood and your world? How could you close your eyes to unredeemed, unforgiven, unrepentant, when you see what sin is doing to distort judgment, twist personalities, and destroy families?

47

Again, in this world, all of us need food, clothing, housing, and many other things. These are purchased with money, and money is often hard to obtain in an amount sufficient for our needs. But trouble is not just local, it is everywhere. Newspaper headlines scream constantly of war, violence and strife between nations; daily they carry stories of atrocities, rape, robbery, corruption in government, catastrophe, murder, greed, violence, injustice. Not to notice and not to care would be to repress the constructive working of a Christian conscience. Of course we care! But we can't let the world and its problems get us down. If we become the victims of unrelieved worry and anxiety, these things can destroy us.

However, many anxieties are of our own making. They come from within, not without. Thousands of folk suffer anxiety because of a guilty conscience. Nothing is calculated to produce sleeplessness more quickly than a condemning conscience. You can't get away from yourself, from what you have been and what you have done until you repent of it and permit Christ to handle it. A guilty conscience needs no accuser, for it furnishes its own. I know a woman who came perilously close to a nervous breakdown by hiding guilt over a period of several years. I know a man whose marriage nearly ended because of the load of guilt he carried and would not confess. The Bible says, "He that covereth his sins will not prosper" (Prov. 28:13, KJV). Don't expect to be relieved of anxiety while sin lies unconfessed and festering in your heart.

A certain woman was living a double life. She really loved her husband but relieved her boredom and loneliness while her husband was away on his frequent business trips by carrying on a clandestine affair with another man. She always felt she could cut off the affair at any time, and really planned to do so. But one day, while her paramour was in the house with her, news came of her husband's death and the door was closed to ever being able to make things right with him. No wonder she became the victim of deep anxiety!

James A. Pike tells of a couple who quarreled rather heatedly one night over a coming visit of the wife's mother. The wife died that·night. Now, their rather violent quarrel took on great new proportions in the husband's mind as he remembered that his last words to his wife were spoken in anger. How much anxiety is caused by careless living and thoughtless speaking!

Would you like to bring anxiety under control and really conquer it? Here are a few suggestions as to how it can be done. First, you must have a clear conscience. Paul told Timothy, his son in the ministry, that he could wage a good spiritual warfare by "holding faith and a good conscience" (1 Tim. 1:19). He also indicated that faith is to be found only when we have a clear conscience (1 Tim. 3:9). In Hebrews 9:14 we read that it takes the blood of Christ to purify conscience and rob it of its condemning power. But, as Paul wrote to Titus, minds and consciences can be corrupted, and when they are you can expect to become the victim of anxiety. If we feel separated from God because of sin, of course we will experience anxiety. But, as we read in 1 John 3:21, "If our heart condemn us not, then we have confidence toward God." And note this word in Hebrews 10:22, "Let us draw near with a true heart in full assurance of faith, having our hearts sprinkled from an evil conscience. . . ." If your conscience is carrying a burden of condemnation, your first step toward peace of mind is to go to God in full confession and repentance. There is no other way to handle this problem.

Second, if you would be free from anxiety, the God in whom you trust must be very real and very great. You must be fully convinced of God's power and ability to take care of you. A vital, strong, living faith in God is absolutely essential to freedom from anxiety. I am reminded of the faith of my own sainted father. What a quiet, unassuming confidence in God was his. He never lost the assurance that God was with him, that God was guiding him, that God would take care of him, and so he was calm when others were excited, confident when others were worried, relaxed when others were tense and afraid. How real and vital is *your* faith in God? Have faith in God, for without faith it is impossible to please him.

Third, to combat anxiety you need a warm, genuine love for God. In Luke 10:27 we read, "Thou shalt love the Lord thy God with all thy heart, and with all thy soul, and with all thy

strength, and with all thy mind: and thy neighbor as thyself.''
Generally speaking, the size of our faith will be determined by
the quality of our love. There is something relaxing in loving
and knowing you are loved in return. The Bible says, ''There is
no fear in love; but perfect love casteth out fear'' (1 John 4:18).
Perfect love casts out anxiety, too, for anxiety is one form of
fear. Anxiety is an uneasiness of the mind, a restless inability to
be at peace. If you love God you will trust him and not be
afraid. Isn't worry evidence that trust is absent?

Fourth, to combat anxiety, we need patience—a great deal of
it. And isn't patience a manifestation of a certain kind of faith?
Patience and anxiety don't mix very well. Patience and piety go
well together. When your trust in God is strong you are able to
wait. New Testament translators often used the words *patience*
and *steadfastness* interchangeably. To cure anxiety let your
allegiance to Christ be as solid as a rock—no wavering, no
vacillating, no inconsistency in your protestations of fidelity and
loyalty. Insincerity will produce anxiety. In Romans 12:12 Paul
exhorted Christians to be ''patient in tribulation.'' This means
giving up to God the trying circumstances of life and the
persecutions which come our way. It means not fretting over
undeserved criticism or wasting time feeling sorry for ourselves.
In Psalm 119:165 we read, ''Great peace have those who love
thy law; nothing can make them stumble'' (RSV). This is the
peace that allays anxiety; it is the trust that cancels fear.

Fifth, to combat anxiety we need a strong confidence in
prayer. Prayer has always played a vital part in the life of every
radiant, victorious Christian. Prayer is conversation with God.
How can anxieties possess you, control you, frighten you, after
you have enjoyed an encouraging, stimulating conversation with
the Lord? When you pray, you are enabled to love. When you
pray, you are able to forgive. When you pray, you find a deep,
calm assurance in God. A woman said recently, ''Last night I
had a terrible fright, but I prayed and all the fear left me.'' In
prayer we give life over into God's keeping, to be lived under
divine control. Job must have been a praying man; otherwise
how could he have said of the Lord, ''Though he slay me, yet
will I trust him (13:15)? We used to sing a song which said,

50

"Take your burden to the Lord and leave it there." Prayer helps us to do this. In prayer you lay at God's feet your anxieties, worries, cares, and fears, and leave them there, knowing that God is perfectly capable of dealing with them. Learn how to *really* pray. Saturate your soul in the spirit of prayer, the spirit of the Bible. Read the holy Word of God, especially the Psalms and the Gospels, until you experience it down deep in your soul. There is healing for mind and soul in his holy Word. Again, live with enthusiasm. Find something worth living for; then give yourself to it with your whole heart.

Trouble? Of course you will have trouble. Everyone has trouble. But when you love the Lord and have faith in him you will understand the fine Christian woman who said, "I just took those troubles in my two hands and put them into the big hands of God, and together we handled them." God and you together *can* handle *anything!* Trust God, won't you? Your anxieties will be dispelled like mists before the rising sun.

R. Eugene Sterner
Christian Brotherhood Hour Speaker
1968-1977

Who Are You?

"From now on, therefore, we regard no one from a human point of view; even though we once regarded Christ from a human point of view, we regard him thus no longer" (2 Cor. 5:16, RSV).

Someone told of how he had carefully watched a singer on television. He said she was wearing a wig, false eyelashes, caps on her teeth, a *heavy* layer of makeup, and an artificial expression. Her first number was "I Gotta Be Me!" He felt like asking, "Well who *are* you? Do you *know* who you are? Are you a real person or just a make-believe?" A great many people really don't know who they are—even those who sing and talk so much about it.

A minister friend of mine related the following story. A very successful business executive, the president of his company, lost his job when the company was merged with a larger company. And he didn't know what to do with himself. He had no real financial worries, but he was terribly unhappy. He really didn't know who he was as a person He had so long identified himself with his responsibilities, his position, and his status, that when that was taken away, he was like a stranger to himself.

A young man had come from a very wealthy family. He had always had anything he wanted—the most expensive clothes, a sports car, and all the other things that go with wealth. Then his father died suddenly, leaving him nothing of his estate. He was suddenly cut off from wealth. But his sense of personhood had always been identified with wealth and a wealthy family. He became desperate. He didn't know who he was as a person. He had no purpose of his own. He had no life work. He was lost.

An intelligent teen-age girl was feeling rebellious and defiant against her father and mother. In her protesting, she had done some things she was not proud of. Talking with her father about this, she groped in her confusion for some understanding of why she felt as she did. "I really don't know why I did that," she told him. "I don't want to hurt you and mother. I've always loved and respected you so much. It's just that all my life I've been nothing but your daughter. I've always tried to do nothing that would hurt your influence or your name. But I wonder what I would be like if I were completely on my own. What are *my* standards? What would I be like it it weren't for you? I really don't know who I am." She was expressing in words what, I suppose, every young person feels to some degree. Each one has to find himself or herself as a person. A child is at first almost completely identified with the family, and the process of growth must be the development of a *personal* identity, a personal sense of vocation and purpose. Young people need to ask themselves, "Who am I? What am I to do with this life of mine?"

Any pastor has faced this basic question with the woman whose companion has been taken from her. She has lived to support him. She has borne his name. She has been his wife, the mother of his children. When she is suddenly left alone, she is faced not only with financial problems but even more with the question of personal identity. She is no longer Mr. Blank's wife. She is a person. She has to find her identity as a person.

The same principle holds when a man retires from an active career. All his working life he had been identified with his position, his work, and his status. Regardless of how well he might have succeeded in his career, he has a period of real adjustment to make when he retires. He has to find himself again, sometimes in new relationships.

There probably is no group more baffled by this problem of personal identity and worthwhileness than the wives of pastors. Across the last twenty-five years or so I have had many conferences with groups of pastor's wives and have counseled with many couples. Not only is a pastor's wife in the position of supporting and assisting her husband in his work, she also is often the buffer between the pastor and his people. People have a way of expecting certain things of her—even demanding them—and she finds herself always trying to meet the expectations of people, yet never quite knowing just what it is that is expected. She has a problem of knowing who *she* really is. It isn't often that a pastor's wife resents her place in life, but it is often confusing to her. Yet her emotional health and happiness depends upon knowing herself under God.

Recently, in a counseling session, this all came very forcibly to me, and my mind went to a passage of Scripture that I previously had passed over too lightly. Here it is from 2 Corinthians 5:16: "From now on, therefore, we regard no one from a human point of view. . . ." The full meaning comes through when you look at different translations of that text. Here are some: "Worldly standards have ceased to count in our estimate of any man" (NEB); Our knowledge of men can no longer be based on their outward lives" (Phillips) or "I estimate no one by what is external" (Moffatt). This is a very interesting passage because it draws a distinction between the way a person may be seen according to "worldly standards" and the way one is seen according to Christian standards. And it comes right to the heart of our question, "Who are you?" To answer that rightly calls for faith in the Creator who made all of us. The Bible says God created man out of the dust of the earth and he became a "living being" or "living soul"—*person!*

Well, what are the "worldly standards" by which we are known? A person is considered to be of value as one is able to produce goods, or make a profit, or acquire wealth, or entertain us, or acquire power or prestige or something else. We are judged by *appearances,* by the *external.* And often we are deceived into taking that judgment as valid and final. Furthermore, we ourselves tend to judge others by outward appearances, by worldly standards.

Now when we accept such false standards, we lose the genius and power of the Christian faith because that faith teaches us not only about God and his requirements, it teaches us about humanity and the real nature of humankind. Jesus came to reveal to us the nature of God and divine love. He came, also, to show us what we can be. Jesus himself was known as the Son of God and as the Son of man—representative of both God and humanity, and uniting in his person both full divinity and full humanity.

Now that puts everything in a different light. A person is *not* to be measured or judged by worldly standards, by position or status or wealth or popularity. God has made each one of us with intrinsic value. God has given each of us a mission and purpose in life. Your value and mine depends upon *whether we live in God's will.* If we don't, all of life is out of kilter for us. If we do, we come alive, truly alive! That's why the person who is truly surrendered to God's will, and faithfully obedient to him is inwardly free and happy, even when that person isn't thought of as important by worldly standards. And the "important" person by worldly standards is so often empty, unhappy, and artificial. You have to do more than sing "I Gotta Be Me." You have to find yourself as a person, in God's will for your life.

This has meaning for Christians as they try to win other people to Christ. Indeed it is in this connection that the Apostle Paul wrote these words to the people at Corinth. If you're going to win people, he said, you have to be controlled by the love of Christ, you have to *see* people in a different way—the Christ-like way, not by worldly standards.

This is a matter that is intensely personal. It makes a world of difference how you see yourself. One minister preached a sermon entitled "Can You Forgive God?" He was talking to those people who feel resentful over what life has dealt them, the people who berate themselves because they don't compare very favorably with others in terms of the worldly standards. He tried to help them see their intrinsic worth as persons and to give back to God their love, trust, devotion, and service. Many people need such a message, for they never have been able to accept themselves.

You, my friend, are an individual person, created by God in his own image. You have potential far beyond what you now can see. You have a God-given purpose, a vocation of your own. If you would find any true happiness and usefulness, you will have to find who *you* really are and surrender yourself to God who made you. Your value is not tied up with position or wealth or status or physical beauty. *Your value is built in.* Then find yourself—in God. You won't be like anybody else, but you can be yourself, under God.

First, receive God's love and forgiveness which covers every sin, every failure, everything false and unworthy. Receive that by faith.

Second, accept yourself, forgiven and cleansed, and thank God for every possibility he has put within you. Begin there with gratitude.

Third, ask God, as Paul the Apostle did, "Lord, what would you have me to do." Open your heart and seek God's will for your life.

Fourth, surrender to God's will. Seek the Lord's will constantly. Be obedient. Let God lead you on *in* his will.

Fifth, refuse to be distracted by what someone else does. You have your own mission to fulfill. When you do this, you will know who you are—and who God is!

God Knows You!

"O Lord, thou hast searched me and known me," cried the psalmist. "Thou knowest when I sit down and when I rise up; thou discernest my thought . . . thou searchest out my path . . . and art acquainted with all my ways" (Ps. 139:1-6, RSV). That text speaks for all of us. The Lord knows much more about us than we ourselves know.

Strange as it may seem, we have a very difficult time understanding ourselves. Thousands of people every week go to psychologists, psychiatrists, psychoanalysts, counselors, and pastors because they don't understand themselves. Sometimes they are encouraged to probe deep into their memories and early experiences in the effort to uncover the source of their feelings and behavior which they themselves don't understand, and which, very often, they abhor. No, we don't understand ourselves very well because there are some things within us which we push down out of consciousness. Then they fester there.

The psalmist, however, had the secret. Standing under the canopy of sky above him, he sensed the searching, probing Spirit of God. How terrifying it would be to know that every thought and feeling, every subtle motive, every human weakness and foible was *known* to a holy God, just and pure—a God who had unlimited power to punish! Terrifying, yes—until you remember that God also is your heavenly Father whose love and mercy is unbounded. Then how wonderful, how perfectly marvelous it is to see that God, while knowing the very worst about you, still loves you with an *unconditional love!* It really is true!

So, what is there to hide? Why try to hide anything? When we really believe in God's love, we can acknowledge the worst in ourselves, and we can rejoice in the fondest dreams we ever have cherished because God knows about them, too. Across the years I have talked with many people suffering from guilt and shame, some who felt their lives were beyond any hope of peace and fulfillment. Like any minister would, I have tried to help these guilt-ridden people to accept God's love and open their lives to him. Some, I'm thankful to say, have done that. And what a difference it made! Tensions melted away. Frowns and worry changed to the smile of peace. It's truly a wonderful thing just to receive God's searching, healing love. It is like sunlight upon the damp musty ground bringing forth vigorous, growing plants. Something happens in the life of persons who open themselves inwardly to God. For God knows us. God knows all about us. God has *searched* us and *known* us.

For one thing, *God knows us physically and humanly.* "For he knows our frame," said the psalmist, "he remembers that we are dust" (103:14). These physical bodies of ours are God's creation. The Bible says that God created man out of the dust of the earth, breathed into his nostrils the breath of life, and man became a living soul, or a living *person.* Now surely God understands the earthly part of us as well as the spiritual part. But it's surprising how many people, sincere and conscientious, have a sense of condemnation and shame about their bodies and their physical urges. It may be due to one's early environment and training, or it may be because of some unfortunate experience. Whatever the cause, we can't go back and change what has already happened. We can, however, accept the fact of God's love. We can start on the road to healing and wholeness. God knows us already—and God loves us.

This does not, by any means, give us a license to do what is wrong. It does not mean we may follow the lusts of the flesh, but it does mean we can have a wholesome view of the physical, human side of our lives. God knows our frame. God remembers that we are dust. I'm glad God knows me as I really am.

God knows our thoughts, too. "Thou discernest my thoughts," says the psalm. "Even before a word is on my tongue, O Lord, thou knowest it altogether" (139:2, 4). We stand before God with no defense, no hiding place, no secrets. No wonder the psalmist cried, "Let the words of my mouth and the meditation of my heart be acceptable in thy sight, O Lord, my rock and my redeemer" (19:14). "Search me," he said, "and know my heart!" Try me and know my thoughts! And see if there be any wicked way in me" (139:23, 24).

That is not a morbid self-examination or ingrown thinking necessarily. The aim of a devout person always is to be clean inside as well as in outward ways. True worship always calls for cleansing. And all of us know that there are areas in our own lives where we need the cleansing, purging, healing power of the Holy Spirit. My own experience has been that of almost constantly seeing where I have needed to measure up. Perhaps I have had more need for inner growth than most people, but how very loving and merciful the Lord has been to lead me gently along the path of self-realization and cleansing. I still have a long way to go too, of course.

Often our greatest problems are personality problems. Our sins are sins of disposition, sins of the spirit. Can we hope to overcome these? If we are to overcome them, it must be by opening the deeper areas of mind and feelings where the problems are. The psalmist gave us the way. It is to open ourselves to the searching, cleansing work of the Holy Spirit. He knows our thoughts and he knows our human weakness. And he still loves us. Isn't that wonderful?

God knows our words. God knows what we say and how we say it. God understands the subtle inflections which convey meanings beyond the words themselves. God takes note of the sarcasm and the condescending tone and can hear a whisper. God knows about slander and is aware of the nuance in meaning that reflects upon another person's good name. God hears the profanity, the blasphemy, the lies—little white lies included.

61

Nothing escapes God's listening ear. But God hears also the note of joy when we speak well of another and knows when we refrain from derogatory comment, even when it would be so easy to add something to what has been said.

Do you ever wish you could recall some things you have said? I do, and I suspect most people do. Aren't you glad that the God who knows every word that we have spoken loves us? As the psalmist said, "Let the words of my mouth . . . be acceptable in thy sight." Some of us need to pray that prayer.

God sees what we do and knows why we do it. God knows what goes on behind doors closed and locked and what is done surreptitously in the secret place. God knows about the shortchanging, the cheating, the shoplifting, and all the rest. There is nothing hidden from the Spirit of God. Aren't you glad that, knowing the worst about you and the most evil deeds you have ever done, God still loves you? God does! And God will forgive the very moment you turn to him in confession.

God knows our path. God knows what lies ahead as well as what is in the past. God has a plan for each life. "Thou searchest out my path," said the psalmist, "and art acquainted with all my ways" (139:3). What a precious and wonderful assurance to know that the God of heaven has a will and a plan for your own life. God knows you. God knows your capacity and ability. You can safely put your life in God's hands. "Trust in the Lord with all your heart," says the proverb, "and do not rely on your own insight. In all your ways acknowledge him, and he will make straight your paths. Be not wise in your own eyes; fear (or reverence) the Lord, and turn away from evil. It will be healing to your flesh and refreshment to your bones" (Prov. 3:5-8).

Yes, God knows you—your physical frame, your humanity, your thoughts, your motives, your words, your deeds. God will bless your sacrifice and will make you a blessing.

Finally, God knows our heartaches, our burdens, our sorrows and frustrations. So many of my listener friends have written to me about their problems and have asked me to pray for them. And I do pray. The consecrated, loving Christian people who work in our office pray. Many of our friends in the listening audience group together regularly to pray with us about these requests which are constantly coming in. Let me assure you that God knows and cares. His people care, too. Believe me, they do.

You there by your radio right now, do you have a problem in your own life? Do you have a burden for someone dear to you? Perhaps a son or daughter has gone astray or a condition in your home brings you grief. Whatever it might be, let me assure you that *God knows you*. Here is a text that has meant so much to me: "Commit your way to the Lord; trust in him, and he will act" (Ps. 37:5).

Lord of All Life

"And Jesus came and said to them, 'All authority in heaven and on earth has been given to me' " (Matt. 28:18, RSV).

There are many Christians who are *forgiven,* but they are not *controlled*; there are many who have accepted Jesus Christ as Savior but have never yielded their lives to him as Lord; there are many who go so far as to believe that, through Christ, they can be right with God but do not go far enough to be caught up in his divine purpose. As a matter of fact you don't hear very much preaching and teaching these days on the lordship of Christ. The result is that often our lives are only neutral and passive. We are not much of a threat to what is evil because we are too content with merely being saved ourselves.

What does the lordship of Christ mean to us? To those who take it seriously it means that all of life—*all of life*—is under his control. It means that his authority in heaven and on earth is real and we live under that authority. Along with his authority there is his divine power to back it up. We, therefore, do not live alone or in our own strength. We are under his authority, his control, and his power if we recognize his lordship and obey him. This is what brings the dimension of depth to your Christian experience. This is what makes the difference between a neutral, passive Christian life and an effective witness for Christ. The person who is forgiven may be saved, but the person who is controlled is *used by God,* and there is no higher privilege than that! Look at the power and authority of Christ and you will find courage as his early followers did.

Jesus Christ is Lord of all creation. John's Gospel declares, "He was in the beginning with God; all things were made through him, and without him was not anything made that was made. In him was life, and the life was the light of men" (John 1:3-4). That's the lordship of the Creator himself. The Apostle Paul saw Christ as "far above all rule and authority and power and dominion, and above every name that is named, not only in this age but also in that which is to come" Furthermore, he declared that Christ "has put all things under his feet" (Eph. 1:21, 22). The same Apostle, writing to the Colossian people, said that Christ "is the image of the invisible God, the first-born of all creation: for in him all things were created, in heaven and on earth, visible and invisible, whether thrones or dominions or principalities or authorities—all things were created through him and for him" (Col. 1:15-16). You see, Christ is Lord over all creation.

Since Christ is Lord over all creation, it follows that he is Lord over the human body. If you study the life of Jesus, you will be nearly overwhelmed by the amount of physical healing that took place in his ministry. They brought to him "all manner of sickness and disease," and he healed them. People with palsy, people who were blind, people who were crippled and never had been able to walk—all these and countless others he healed. He simply spoke the word of authority and it was done.

And this has happened since, too. He promised his followers that such works would continue in his name. Here's what he said: "Truly, truly, I say to you, he who believes in me will also do the works that I do; and greater works than these will he do, because I go to the Father. Whatever you ask in my name, I will do it, that the Father may be glorified in the Son" (John 14:12-13).

Jesus Christ is Lord over the elements of nature. In some marvelous way unknown to us, he transcended the laws of nature and affirmed his lordship over them. When a violent storm arose on the Sea of Galilee, he calmed the tempest with

65

his word, "Peace, be still." The disciples were awestruck with all this, saying, "Even the winds and the sea obey him." But if he is the Lord of creation, this would be expected. When several thousand people had followed him up along the mountainside—many of them hungry—he called for a few small loaves and fishes from a mere boy and multiplied them into sufficient food to feed the multitude. How could that be? Well, who knows? We do not understand it. We simply call it a miracle. But the Lord of all creation is Lord of the elements in it. That isn't all strange in the light of his lordship.

Christ is Lord of space. There is no such thing as distance with him. When an official came to him asking that he come to Capernaum to heal his son, Jesus simply said, "Go, your son will live." The man believed him and returned home. And before he reached his own house some of his servants came running to tell him that his son was well. Checking the time that his son began to mend, he found it was the very time the Lord Jesus had given him the word that he was healed.

In January 1971, I was on a preaching tour in the Caribbean area and South America. At one point, I was in a very difficult and dangerous spot and saw so clearly the hand of God at work. When I returned home my daughter told me that while I was gone she had awakened from sleep with a great burden for me. She had gotten out of bed, knelt down and prayed for me until the burden was lifted. We checked on the time and found that at the very time I was in need, she had been burdened for me. I have no doubt whatever that God spoke to her. With the Lord there is no space. God is Lord of all.

Jesus Christ is Lord over the Law. We know, of course, that the people of his day were sticklers for the Law. Ceremonial laws were extremely important to them. Legalism was a binding, condemning thing. Religion was a burden. Jesus asserted his lordship over that. When his disciples rubbed out the heads of wheat in their hands on the Sabbath, they were severely condemned by the Pharisees, but Jesus called their attention to the higher law of love and concern for persons. "I tell you," he said, "something greater than the temple is here. And if you had known what this means, 'I desire mercy, and not sacrifice,' you would not have condemned the guiltless. For the Son of man is lord of the sabbath" (Matt. 12:1-8). What a liberating thing that is! The higher law of love in Christ is the law of the Lord of creation.

Jesus Christ is Lord of life and death. He took a girl by the hand and lifted her up. New life came into her body. Death was, to him, only sleeping. He is Lord over sin and death and the grave. He himself, crucified on the hideous Roman cross, expiring there in the heat of the day, was raised up from the grave, electrifying the whole city and giving hope to the whole world. This power over death has changed our whole outlook. We can have hope.

Jesus raised Lazarus from the dead after he had been in the grave four days. There was no limit to his authority. If you take the account seriously, you have to recognize a tremendous power over the Creation itself and over all the physical world. He employed spiritual laws which transcended and short-cut the laws of nature and the physical world. This gives promise of our own future in him. No wonder the Apostle Paul wrote to the Romans this way: "If the Spirit of him who raised Jesus from the dead dwells in you, he who raised Christ Jesus from the dead will give life to your mortal bodies also through his Spirit which dwells in you" (Rom. 8:11).

Jesus Christ is Lord over the very power of evil, over Satan himself. Time after time he cast the demons out of afflicted, tormented people. The maniac among the tombs was but one example. Mary Magdalene was transformed from the tyranny of the evil one and became a lovely, loyal follower of Jesus. She stood by at his crucifixion and was first at the tomb on that first Easter morning.

"Now is the judgment of this world," Jesus said, "now shall the ruler of this world be cast out; and I, when I am lifted up from the earth, will draw all men to myself" (John 12:31). The power of evil is broken by the authority of Jesus Christ. When he went to the cross, he became the object of our hope forever. Just before he left those awestricken followers, he said, "All authority in heaven and on earth has been given to me. Go therefore and make disciples of all nations . . ." (Matt. 28:18-19).

Jesus Christ is our Savior, and he is our Lord. He has provided for our salvation and he also claims our lives as our living Lord. It is not enough to be forgiven, precious as that is. Jesus Christ is Lord! "None of us lives to himself," wrote the Apostle, "and none of us dies to himself. If we live, we live to the Lord, and if we die, we die to the Lord; so then, whether we live or whether we die, we are the Lord's. For to this end Christ died and lived again, that he might be Lord both of the dead and of the living" (Rom. 14:7-9).

Each year we hear the *Messiah*, the superb oratorio written by George Frederick Handel. I never cease to marvel at the power and beauty of that masterpiece. When the choir comes to the "Hallelujah Chorus" with its "King of kings and Lord of lords," my heart nearly bursts with joy and praise. When they sing, "He shall reign forever and ever," my soul cries out within me, "Let it be so in my heart." Live or die, I am the Lord's. How about you?

The Gifts of the Spirit in Perspective

"As each has received a gift, employ it for one another, as good stewards of God's varied grace: whoever speaks, as one who utters oracles of God; whoever renders service, as one who renders it by the strength which God supplies; in order that in everything God may be glorified through Jesus Christ. To him belong glory and dominion forever and ever. Amen" (1 Pet 4:10-11, RSV).

You hear a great deal these days about the gifts of the Holy Spirit. This probably sounds mysterious to some people, but to Bible students it is language well understood. The New Testament clearly teaches that the Holy Spirit endows people with spiritual gifts for the purpose of carrying on the ministry entrusted to them by the Lord Jesus Christ.

But there is confusion over this now. On the one hand there are those who talk glibly about their own experience as though that experience had become the standard for everybody. On the other hand there are many who are afraid of the whole business and make no room for spontaneous spiritual gifts at all. As a result, a great many churches have been divided and confused. Sometimes it's hard to tell where the cause of the division really is. The purpose of this message is to set spiritual gifts in proper perspective and relationship. Let me make several basic observations.

First, we have to accept the whole, full-orbed ministry of the Holy Spirit. Some have declared that certain gifts of the Spirit are no longer needed and no longer valid, but they simply do not have any authority or right to declare any of these gifts as no longer valid. The gifts of the Spirit are given as the Spirit wills. The initiative is with him, not with us.

Furthermore, the Church *needs* the full ministry of the Holy Spirit in every age and every generation. We cannot carry on the work of the Lord ourselves. The Holy Spirit is given by God to teach us, to lead us, to enable us, and empower us for this service. If we deny the Spirit, we make the church a helpless cripple before a society that desperately needs God's saving power. No, you cannot deny any of the gifts of the Spirit by your own arbitrary decision. He gives these gifts as he wills. Here is what the Scripture says: "All these (gifts) are inspired by one and the same Spirit, who apportions to each one individually as he wills" (1 Cor. 12:11). Let's say it again, loud and clear. We need the full, whole ministry of the Holy Spirit through God's people.

The gifts of the Holy Spirit are given for the edification and the usefulness of the whole fellowship. What we hear so much about now is the individual experience. It almost seems that the gift a person claims is used to enhance one's own prestige and set one apart as more spiritual than the others. But the New Testament clearly teaches that such a gift is given "for the common good" (1 Cor. 12:7). In the first letter from the Apostle Peter this is made very clear. "As each has received a gift, employ it for one another, as good stewards of God's varied grace: whoever speaks, as one who utters oracles of *God;* whoever renders service, as one who renders it by the strength which *God* supplies; in order that in everything God may be glorified through Jesus Christ. To him belong glory and dominion forever and ever. Amen" (1 Pet. 4:10-11).

There are some basic points in this passage (1) A gift is to be employed as a blessing for others. (2) It is to be exercised by you as a steward—that is, it is not yours. You are only the steward of it. (3) It is to be exercised by God's grace and not of ourselves. (4) It is that "in everything God may be glorified through Christ,'' for the way we glorify God is by glorifying the Son. Now that doesn't sound much like the preening self-righteousness you sometimes see, does it? That's what I mean by setting this whole business in the proper perspective and relationship. According to this text, we are stewards of God's "varied" grace. That means God's many different expressions of grace, or we may say, God's many gifts. God works in so many different ways through so many different people, it really isn't very appropriate for any one of us to feel exalted.

It is in the fellowship that the blessing of each person's ministry is conserved and multiplied. We all depend upon one another. Take time to read Romans 12 and see how the fellowship is compared to the human body with every member depending on the others. We belong together. We help correct and balance one another.

A gift of the Holy Spirit is not the same as a natural ability or talent, and yet you cannot really separate the two altogether. Someone has defined a spiritual gift as a natural ability or capacity that has been taken over by the Holy Spirit and has "caught fire." That definition is hardly adequate, though, because quite often God has used, in a remarkable way, those who seemed to have little or no natural ability in that direction. Some of those twelve men who became apostles would be good illustrations. They certainly didn't look like apostles at first. I have seen people who emerged from seemingly nothing into even great leadership.

A gift of the Spirit then, is more than merely the development of natural abilities, though very often it seems God takes the natural ability, uses it, enhances it, and expands it into much more than a natural ability. How can you explain a D. L. Moody or Ira Sankey or Charles Spurgeon or John Wesley in terms of human ability? You can't! God took such consecrated men as Paul the Apostle and Martin Luther, and lifted them out of themselves. God used their natural capacities, of course, but God gave to them a quality and usefulness far beyond that. That is a spiritual gift.

All the gifts of the Spirit are important in their proper place. We make a mistake to exalt certain functions out of proportion. As I speak now about gifts of the Spirit, I am aware that many of my listeners will be hung up, thinking about just one or two. Many will be sidetracked right now on the subject of speaking in tongues. Why? Because that's what we have heard so much about. Others will be thinking of the gift of prophecy. Why? Because that's what has been so prominent in the life of the Church for so long. But there must be almost unlimited expressions of God's "varied grace." The lists of spiritual gifts you see in the letters to the Corinthians, the Romans, and the Ephesians surely are not exhaustive lists. There surely are many ways beyond these that God works through people. How sad it is that so much of the Church has reduced its ministry to the activity of just a few—the preacher, the singer, the teacher—rather than encouraging each person to seek a gift of usefulness and blessing. God wants to work through all of the people so that it can be said now as it was to the church at Ephesus: There is "one God and Father of us all, who is above all and through all and in all," with "grace . . . given to each of us according to the measure of Christ's gift" (Eph. 4:6-7). So it is that "God arranged the organs in the body, each one of them, as he chose" (1 Cor. 12:18).

The gifts of the Spirit are to glorify Jesus Christ. Jesus himself made this very clear when he was speaking to his disciples about the ministry of the Holy Spirit. "He will glorify me," he said, "for he will take what is mine and declare it to you" (John 16:15). So Christ is to be in the focus of attention and devotion. The spotlight is to be on him, not on us at all. If we obey the Holy Spirit, we shall be glorifying Christ in everything.

This means also that if you are obedient in the exercising of your gift, whatever it may be, you will be called upon to carry your cross. It means, not self-centeredness but self-giving. That's what it meant for Jesus. The exercise of his divine gifts led to a cross. Back in those days and nights of trial and testing in the wilderness, he resisted every temptation to a cheap use of those divine gifts. We will have to make the same decisions about the use of what God gives to us.

We are always choosing whether we will take the safe, easy way of well-planned, well-organized, well-defined institutions in the Church, or whether we will dare to open ourselves to the dynamic, biblical meanings and to the gifts of the Holy Spirit which just might upset some of our neat arrangements sometimes. Much of the institutional church makes little or no room for the spontaneous expression of the Holy Spirit and the gifts of the Spirit in God's people. With all our plans made, all our methods selected, all our people primed, and all our organizational activities defined, we don't really feel much need for the Holy Spirit. Then along comes the unstructured, undefined, non-descript group with lots of spontaneous expression and we don't know how to handle it. Wouldn't it be wonderful if we could bring new life and spontaneity into the organized institution, providing room for the gifts of the Spirit? Right there, I suspect, is the real challenge to the Church.

Where do you fit into all this? Are you ready for God to use you for divine glory? Do you feel that he has given you a spiritual gift? Remember God works through the whole body of people. God is not calling you to go off on a tangent. God is calling you to become a vital, glowing, witnessing, serving person right in and through the Church.

One in the Bonds of Love

"Behold, how good and how pleasant it is when brothers dwell in unity" (Ps. 133:1, RSV).

The warmest and most sacred bond known to human beings is the loving relationship of a truly Christian family. And the next most sacred must surely be that of Christian believers who are one in the bonds of love. What a beautiful experience it is to be a part of the caring fellowship. Some of us know what that means, especially in times of tragedy or bereavement or sickness. Hundreds of times I have seen groups of Christian people share the burdens of others—praying, giving, encouraging, supporting. And as I have observed such caring love in action, the words of the psalmist have come alive once more: "Behold, how good and how pleasant it is when brothers dwell in unity" (Ps. 133:1).

And this reaches out far beyond the local congregation. Across my mind right now there marches a whole procession of beautiful and precious memories, images of wonderful persons, and experiences of caring fellowship never to be forgotten. It has been such a privilege to know many Christian brothers and sisters in other lands. Different languages, different cultures, different customs, but one in the bonds of love. Likewise, it has been deeply rewarding to know and work with fellow Christians in various groups and denominations. Different beliefs at some points, different ways of worship perhaps, but one in the bonds of love. To use the words of one noted leader, these are days when the denominational walls are crumbling and believers are finding one another.

Some great efforts have been made to bring about unity among Christians by the merging of denominational organizations and by federations of various sorts, but those who have been most active at that know very well that real unity does not take place until there are bonds of love and caring. That doesn't take place at the high arches of ecclesiastical mergers but at the grass roots of loving service and sharing.

How the great heart of our Lord Jesus must have yearned as he prayed for his disciples and for all believers. "I do not pray for these only," he cried, "but also for those who are to believe in me through their word, that they may all be one; even as thou, Father, art in me, and I in thee, that they also may be in us, so that the world may believe that thou hast sent me" (John 17:20-21). He prayed for their unity, but he defined the kind of unity—"as thou, Father, are in me, and I in thee, that they also may be in us" Phillips translates that this way: "Just as you, Father, live in me and I live in you." You see, it is the *sharing of his life* that brings unity. It is not on the basis of all seeing "eye to eye," but on the basis of being *in him*. Jesus didn't say that people would know us as his disciples because we all agreed on every fine point; he said, "By this all men will know that you are my disciples, if you have love for one another" (John 13:35).

Now, let's get down to some specifics. Suppose you and I disagree on some point of doctrine. What shall we do? Reject each other? argue? If we each try to prove the other wrong we probably will end up farther apart. But if we open God's Word to seek and learn together we probably will end up closer together. Suppose we still don't see alike. Do you expect me to profess agreement with you and conform to your expectations? Or should I make such demands of you? Which shall it be? Or should we respect and honor each other as honest human beings and as Christians? Do you have any right to ask me to compromise my integrity in order to conform? Or vice versa? If we love each other Christianly, there's something deeper to bind us together *while* we seek and learn together.

Or suppose we have different ways of worshiping. If people come among us who do not fit in with our customs what shall we do with them? If they conform to our patterns without sincerely meaning what they say or do, are they not being false? How could one be a growing Christian merely by conforming? No, we have to keep integrity and act sincerely or we suffer spiritually. Conforming can be deadening. It can be insincere and false. If unity must be at the price of integrity and honesty, then it's on a false foundation and it will soon crumble. Real unity must be on the basis of personal spiritual growth. It must allow for diversity.

That's why rigid creedalism is wrong. It demands a surrender of personal thinking and responsibility. That's why mere conformity is wrong. It paralyzes personal growth and produces an artificial kind of unity. That's why Jesus gave us a different basis for unity—to be *in him,* united in love.

When I was a very young Christian, I was a member of a local church where the pressures were pretty strong. There were certain things you were to do in a certain way. There were considered "spiritual." I tried it for a little while but I felt false inside. And, being a Pennsylvania Dutchman, I rebelled. It was too great a price to pay for social approval. I had to be me, not somebody else. If I were to be a growing person, I first had to become a real person, honest with myself and with others. I tried not to offend other people and hurt them, of course. I sometimes had to keep my thoughts to myself. I found that you don't always have to say everything you think, though being as outspoken as I am, that was difficult. (For many years I had very few unexpressed thoughts!) Somehow, I managed to get along remaining fairly free to think and grow and become.

This is what I love so much about the Church of God fellowship. I am free to search God's Word, to let it say what it says, and to speak my own convictions. On the Christian Brotherhood Hour, I have had freedom. I do not pretend to speak for all my colleagues. They don't demand that. They speak for themselves. I do learn much from them, and I need them very much. I especially appreciate those of real biblical scholarship. I respect them all deeply, and I feel that they respect my freedom. It's a beautiful relationship and one to be cherished. At the same time, I sense no areas of any significant disagreement. The Bible, after all, is not so obscure unless you get lost in trivial things or in a wilderness of words.

You see, to have unity we have to trust one onother, and we have to trust God to take care of the Church. After all, who has the right to set up ecclesiastical rules to govern God's people? Who has the right to set up standards for others? The Lord has done that. Let's just teach his standard as responsibly as we can and let every person be responsible to think and grow. We don't have to cram everyone into a tight little mold where each one recites like a parrot what is supposed to be said. Jesus would never have approved of that. His greatest *conflict* was with the legalists and the religious rulers who tried to do just that. They were not stimulating people to spiritual growth. They were crushing them by a heavy load of scrupulosities and technical rules.

If we are ever to experience the unity for which Christ prayed we will have to move beyond fear and distrust and legalistic bondage to a relationship of trust and love and true Christian freedom. If you will study the writings of the Apostle Paul, you will see that he was a champion of responsible freedom. "You were called to freedom, brethren," he wrote to the believers at Galatia, "only do not use your freedom as an opportunity for the flesh, but through love be servants of one another. For the whole law is fulfilled in one word, 'You shall love your neighbor as yourself' " (Gal. 5.13-14). Instead of being permissiveness, love is responsibility and caring. The Apostle well knew that there were real differences among the people in those churches. There were Gentiles who had come from the worship of idols and whose manner of life had been immoral. Serious problems arose from these differences, but Paul insists upon responsible Christian freedom. There were risks involved, of course, but here was the basic meaning of the gospel.

The key, then, is Christian love. And love means caring. It means respect for one another. It means a relationship that is greater than having your name on the membership roll of a religious organization. It is entering into a relationship with other persons because you have entered into a relationship with Christ. As Jesus said, it is to be *in* him, in his spirit and purpose, to share in his life. That puts you in a special relationship of love with his people all around the world, for when you belong to Christ, you belong to all those who belong to Christ.

Your Greatest Investment

"He saved others; he cannot save himself" (Matt. 27:42, RSV).

What they said as they stood around the Roman cross where Jesus was crucified was intended as bitter sarcasm and irony: "He saved others; he cannot save himself" (Matt. 27:42). It was the unfolding of a great truth of life. How could he have saved himself and still have saved others? "The chief priests, with the scribes and elders mocked him. . . ." They unknowingly spoke a truth that they themselves had utterly overlooked in all their profession of religion, for they were very busy saving themselves and their institutions. It was just because they were defending themselves that they wanted Jesus crucified. He was disturbing their little system. They couldn't understand self-giving. But self-giving was the very heart of Jesus' message and mission. "God . . . gave his only son." Christ "came not to be ministered unto but to minister and to give his life a ransom for many." So, they said it correctly, even though they themselves didn't understand what they said. "He saved others; he cannot save himself." No one can save others by saving himself. Every great person has been great by giving.

But the giving really turns out to be investment. That was supremely true of Jesus of course, but it has been true in some degree of many people. Those who have given themselves to a truly worthy cause have invested in the future and in the lives of others. Only the years can reveal the returns on their investment.

This was brought forcibly to my mind recently by a listener friend of mine in England. John Godwin, headmaster of a school in Lichfield, Staffordshire, sent me his brief biographical sketches on the lives of certain outstanding persons who, as he put it, "toiled for Christ."

There was Dietrich Bonhoeffer for one. In 1933 when Adolf Hitler came to power in Germany, Bonhoeffer was one of the few to see the evil in his design and the sinister hatred of the Jewish people. When he opposed the Hitler reign of terror, he was repeatedly questioned and threatened, but his great spirit could not be broken. In a concentration camp with all its atrocities he wrote observations that some of us find simply unforgettable. He taught us the meaning of commitment. Just before he paid with his life, he wrote, "This is the end—for me the beginning." He could not save himself, but he invested powerfully in the cause of right and truth the world over.

There was William Booth who, assisted by his wife Catherine, gathered together a group of helpers to assist them in reaching the down-and-out for Christ. He called his small group the Salvation Army. Together they went the limit to help the people who were really in need. Often they suffered ridicule and abuse; sometimes they were pelted by aroused mobs. But the movement spread, first in England, then in other countries. Who could even begin to estimate the vast good work of the Salvation Army? They could not save themselves and still save others. William and Catherine Booth still live in countless thousands of lives that have been touched by that ministry of mercy.

Louis Braille was another who gave himself. Louis lost his sight when he was three years old. At the age of ten he was sent to a school for the blind where he learned to read using books with raised letters. But that method was very clumsy and slow. He heard of a system being used by the French army, a system of dots and dashes. With that basic concept he worked on the principle of six dots in various combinations that could be fit underneath a fingertip. These, in raised dots, could be felt quickly with the finger. The result was what is now called the Braille system. While Louis Braille died at the early age of 43, he left behind a precious legacy to those people who walk in the darkness of blindness. He gave himself. He didn't pity himself. He invested himself in others, leaving a legacy for generations to come.

One could go on and on with such a list. Civilization has moved forward on the feet of those people who have given themselves, who creatively used their opportunity, and even their adversity, to bless and lift other people. They invested their energy, and we still reap the dividends on their investment. Helen Keller brought a sense of beauty to countless others though she herself was cut off from sight and sound. Beethoven gave to the world some of its most sublime and immortal music which he himself, being stone deaf, could never hear.

Somewhere I read that Booker T. Washington, deprived and poor, walked hundreds of miles to one of the very few universities which, at that time, would admit a black student. Even when he got there, he was told that all classes were full. Offered a job making beds and sweeping floors, he made those beds more neatly and swept those floors cleaner than they ever had been. Eventually he was taken into some of the classes where he distinguished himself for intelligence and dedication. He went on to become a fine scholar and an outstanding administrator in education. Booker T. Washington will always stand as a symbol of self-giving. He didn't pity himself. He invested himself, and thousands today profit from his investment.

We who are parents understand this. Our major investment is in our children. Some of you may have stocks and bonds and savings accounts; all of them are investments. Your home, if you own one, is an investment. It represents a great deal of work and saving, a great deal of care and maintenance. But you have no investment that even approaches your investment effort and sacrifice, love and understanding, care and nurture in the lives of your children. Mothers especially understand this. Their very hearts have gone into their children. If you are anything like we are at our house, there is no point from which such great rewards in joy and satisfaction have come. I haven't added up the financial investment we have made in our three daughters—their food, clothing, shelter, education, and so on—and I don't plan to. Whatever it amounted to, it's the best investment we ever made.

Years ago I worked rather frequently with a certain funeral director who became a warm friend as well. Once on a long ride, leading a funeral procession for some thirty-five miles, he told me the interesting story of his childhood and youth. His parents had come to America from one of the European countries, arriving on these shores shortly before he was born. His father was an uneducated and very poor man. His mother was from a family a little more affluent and when she received a small inheritance from her family, she used it all to buy tickets for the voyage to this country. When they arrived, they were without friends. He told me of how his father found the simplest, humblest rental quarters and began seeking work in people's yards to buy food. Then he found a regular job, though the pay was very meager. He worked hard, my friend told me, his eyes getting wet. Early and late, with hard manual labor, he managed to sustain the family. My friend's earliest memories were of warm love in a humble home, of family worship, of trusting faith. When he was through elementary school, they found a way to keep him free to go to high school. Then, because he was interested in becoming a funeral director, they insisted that he get the necessary training. Just about the time he had completed his preparation, his father died, with these words to his son: "I have never been much. I haven't been able to do anything very important. . But maybe you can." By the time my friend had finished, the tears were running down his cheeks, and he didn't seem to be one bit embarrassed by it.

His story could be told in other versions by many people. How very much we owe to our parents. They have invested their very lives in us. It does seem appropriate that we appreciate it and give them the honor and love they deserve. One of the heartbreaking stories I hear and read in letters so much is from parents who have poured their love and their lives into their children only to be rejected and reviled by them later.

When you give yourself, you always take a risk. What if you are later ridiculed? What if it is not appreciated? That's just the risk Jesus took. Not all have accepted him. Some have blasphemed him, but it was to their own shame—not his. He had no choice. We have no choice if we follow him. "He saved others; he could not save himself. . . . He came unto his own, and his own received him not, But as many as received him, to them gave he power to become the sons of God" (Matt. 27:42; John 1:11-12, KJV).

Steady Now!

"A faithful man will abound with blessing, but he who hastens to be rich will not go unpunished" (Prov. 28:20, RSV).

Have you ever stood beside a great engine and watched the flywheel? I used to do that when I was a boy, sometimes going with my father to the station where he worked. There were seven or eight huge one-cylinder engines that pumped gas out to the surrounding towns. I used to wonder why those great, heavy flywheels had to be on there, constantly whirling, as the engine cracked with its monotonous regularity. Then it was explained to me that with the flywheel absorbing the bursts of power and distributing that power smoothly, it not only provided a constancy of power but kept it, the engine, from tearing itself apart with the explosions in the combustion chamber. The *spurts* of power had to be distributed. They had to be smoothed out.

Let's take another illustration. Have you ever paid attention to the apparatus that pumps oil out of the well? You see the beam going up and down, up and down. It always reminds me of the head of a bird trying to find a worm. You will notice the wheel constantly and slowly turning is weighted heavily on one side so it is very much out of balance. But you will see that the heavy side of the wheel is going down while the pump is laboring to lift the load of oil. It is intended to equalize the load on the engine and thus ease the strain. The purpose is to smooth out and distribute the power.

A farmer who raises food and grain always has some means of preserving the harvest and distributing its benefits over the whole year. Otherwise his family would eat only at harvest time. He puts grain in the granary. His wife may be proficient in canning fruit. He may smoke or freeze meat so it will keep. He distributes the intake of the harvest so that they can live well throughout the year.

As you suspect, I intend to draw a lesson from these illustrations. It is this: The best measure of your Christian life is in constancy, the faithfulness and the discipline of your energies rather than in the sudden, shocking experiences. "It is better," as Emerson once said, "that joy should be spread over all the day in the form of strength, than it should be concentrated into ecstasies, full of danger and followed by reactions." Some people measure the Christian life by high moments of ecstasy. But these often are followed by periods of discouragement and depression. To put it in graphic terms, the true measure is not by the "peaks" of the line on your graph but by the slow steady climb of true growth. There will be an unsteady and irregular line, for none of us grows with absolute consistency, but if you backed off for a look at the whole line, you ought to find it gradually climbing. The business executive charts production or sales over the longer period of time, and the wise Christian will not measure growth by feelings at this or that particular moment. But thankful for the times of inspiration and meaningful worship, the wise Christian will seek to let that inspiration permeate all the days and bring affirmation to high resolves. You can't always have the spurts of power. You need the "flywheel" of constancy, of discipline, and of faithfulness to level out the power.

My heart beat a little faster recently as I meditated on Proverbs 28:20. "A faithful man will abound with blessings." And I remembered with joy a passage in Revelation 2:10: ". . . Be faithful unto death, and I will give you the crown of life." The rewards of the faithful person will come, even though they are not experienced every day. As Disraeli put it, "The secret of success is constancy."

These are days when personal experience—especially the spectacular or mystical experience is very popular. Our whole religious climate seems to be saying, "This is how I feel." We seek to outdo one another in relating the unusual experience. For many years this was lacking and there was very little but dry, pedantic theological sermons which left people unmoved. We know that. But perhaps now we have swung to the other extreme. In any case our purpose here is to include both the high moments of experience and the disciplines of thought and action. The spurts of power and inspiration, with the flywheel of regular Christian practices, give continuity and smoothe the power throughout life and conduct. Let me suggest a few basic requirements for this.

First, strive always to be faithful to the best that you know of God's law and of your Christian duty. However you may feel at any moment, this obligation remains the same. If your attention is upon your own feeling, and if you do your duty only when you feel inspired, then you will very frequently find excuse to be unfaithful. But if, while thanking God for your best moments, you carry out your Christian duty, then even greater inspiration will be yours. Accept the fact that duty is duty regardless of feelings. If you are faithful to what you know, then you can have a good conscience and deep satisfaction even in the regular course of things, and you will have a solid basis for new high moments of worship. If you faithfully study the Scriptures, you will find that what you learn and meditate upon will return to you at the most unexpected time as a bright realization. If you practice a life of prayer, even when you don't much feel like praying, you will one day suddenly come into greater meanings in prayer. God rewards faithfulness.

Second, strive always to be faithful in loving. Now we don't always feel loving. There are the times when everything seems to go wrong, when others get on our nerves and we feel confused. Can we still love at those times? Yes, but only by the grace of God. We still can *do* the loving thing even though we don't have effusive feelings. Anyway, love is something we do. It often is an act of the will. But—and here's the beauty of it—if we continue to act loving regardless of our feelings, we will have a greater reward. Having done the loving thing, our feelings soon follow.

Third, strive to be faithful in the work to which God has called you. According to the New Testament, every one of us is called. You think of a preacher as being called, but every Christian is called. Each of us is to serve God in the way for which he or she is fitted, and according to God's will. Now, it is truly a wonderful day when you find God's will for your own life and fulfill your own calling. There is a constant solid reward and satisfaction greater and more lasting than any high moment of inspiration.

Fourth, strive to be faithful in your study of the Scriptures. It simply isn't possible to describe the resources you put deep in your mind and soul when regularly you let the Scripture speak to you. When you plant God's Word in your mind and heart, it becomes for you the living word. Just when you need it, the promise of God comes to your aid and speaks to your condition. What is, at first, merely an idea in your mind becomes a realization in your heart. And power comes into your life.

Fifth, strive to be faithful in relating to your fellow Christians. As Christians we are part of a team. We need one another. We ought to be faithful to the work of the Lord in our own place, to give as well as to receive. Those who forsake their own place of worship to go elsewhere for some special inspiration are giving away the secret that their motive is chiefly to receive, not to give. Christianity is giving, not just receiving. You will find that much of the strength and inspiration you need will come to you through your Christian friends.

Back on our small Pennsylvania farm, I used to take some pride in handling a team of powerful horses. The greatest thrill came when I could get them to pull with all their might. With the reins held moderately taut and speaking to them firmly and gently, I have seen them actually almost crouch and their great bodies tremble as they exerted every ounce of their strength to pull the load. *Steady* is the word. *Steady* and *together*. If one lunged ahead, and then the other lunged, the load didn't move. But steady and together it moved. You are not alone. You can't pull the load alone. Neither can I. Neither can anyone else. God works through people. We belong together. We help one another. Let's pull together!

The measure of the Christian life is not in the ecstatic moments but in the faithful, steady practice of Christian disciplines. Then the inspiration will permeate all your days. It takes the flywheel to spread the explosions out into steady power.

Anxiety—the Killer

"Rejoice in the Lord always; again I will say, Rejoice. Let all men know your forbearance. The Lord is at hand. Have no anxiety about anything, but in everything by prayer and supplication with thanksgiving let your requests be made known to God. And the peace of God, which passes all understanding, will keep your hearts and your minds in Christ Jesus" (Phil. 4:4-7, RSV).

As someone said, "It isn't the motion that wears out a machine—it's the friction." It isn't the activity that wears us out nearly so much as it is the inner tension and anxiety. Some people are tied up in such tight little knots that they are virtually canceled out so far as any real usefulness is concerned. Their health may be impaired, and their happiness very limited. Anxiety can be a killer. Any doctor can tell you of its effect on the whole body, mind, and emotions.

Temporary periods of anxiety, as one is faced with serious problems or decisions, would have to be considered normal. But when one is filled with anxiety most or all of the time, the result can be serious. All of us have anxious times, of course, but we don't have to accept anxiety as a way of life. Up to a certain point, anxiety can be creative, spurring us to greater achievement—the anxiety of an athlete in the tight contest, for instance, or the anxiety that a public speaker feels just before giving an address. But if you feel anxious most or all of the time it can seriously impair your usefulness and happiness.

Well, what is the cause of such anxiety? Or, more accurately, what are the causes, for there are many. In general, anxiety is caused by too much concern about ourselves, what other people think of us, and how we compare with what we expect of ourselves or what others expect of us. Often it is because we don't see ourselves realistically, because we have false images of what we are or what we ought to be and do.

Take, for instance, the boy who grows up with his parents demanding of him more than he can do. He is belittled and humiliated because he doesn't make straight A's in school like his brilliant sister, or doesn't make the football team like his older brother. With an artificial standard imposed upon him, he never really knows himself and his own abilities. He lives in anxiety because he is trying to live by a false standard. Many parents who have expected their children to act like adults have produced anxiety-ridden personalities.

Anxiety is produced when a person has been made to feel guilty over what really is normal. Thousands of people have grown up feeling dirty and sinful just because they were human, physical, sexual beings. They never can quite accept themselves in their humanness. Often religion has been associated with that denial of their humanity, and so its effect is negative rather than positive. It produces anxiety rather than trust and often hostility rather than love. True religion is not permissive and loose, but neither is it life-denying. Jesus Christ was a wholesome, vital human being as well as the Son of God. It is worth noting that God chose to express his very nature *through human flesh*. You don't have to be superhuman. You are not an angel with a halo. Neither am I. We can overcome much of our anxiety by just being realistic and honest about ourselves. This is not to approve and condone what is sinful but it is to say that humanity, as such, is not sinful. God made us the human beings we are. Surely, then, we are not condemned for that. Anxiety is the result of unrealistic demands made upon ourselves.

But on the other hand, anxiety also goes along with guilt over doing what we know full well we should not or failing to do what we know we should. Sometimes there is a deep guilt because wrong has been glossed over or covered up. "He that covereth his sins shall not prosper" says the proverb, and there is profound wisdom in that. Psychiatrists and personal counselors could give you countless examples of hidden guilt that resulted in various forms of anxiety and fear. There is often the fear of being found out. It must get pretty tiresome to always be covering your tracks.

The Philippian letter said, "Have no anxiety about anything, but in everything by prayer and supplication with thanksgiving let your requests be made known to God" (4:6). This suggests an open heart and mind that is not hiding something in anxiety but is full of joyful praise. What a wonderful experience it is just to confess everything to God, to accept his great, unconditional love and grace, to straighten up your past as much as possible, apologize for your wrong, and know that your heart is clean before God and others. The anxiety and fear of being known is gone when you accept God's love in its fullness.

But so many people do not face the reality. They find false ways of dealing with their anxiety or guilt. Here are just some of those false ways. I spell them out because it is important to recognize the deception and futility of them.

First, you can deny that you have the anxiety and push it down out of sight. You can just refuse to face it. Some people push it down so far within them that they actually don't consciously remember it. But it is still there, and it is like poison in the system or a kind of low-grade infection. It keeps festering and tormenting. The more painful something is to face, the more likely one is to repress it. See how foolish and wrong it is? You can see that God's way is right. Confess it. Get it out of your system. Open yourself to divine love and grace. Let the sun shine into the dark, damp, musty corners of your being. It will bring peace and healing and release!

Another false way of dealing with your anxiety is to avoid it, to postpone the confrontation with yourself. Procrastinate. Put it off. Keep running. So many people are running from something inside themselves. They move from one job to another, from one marriage to another, or from one church to another, always seeking something but never quite finding it. They seek the ideal job but they are always disappointed. They seek the euphoric, ideal marriage and romance but there's something wrong with each marriage partner. They are looking for the ideal church but they never contribute much of anything anytime, anywhere. They just keep trotting around. Now you never gain much by running or by postponing or by avoiding the real source of a problem. That only compounds the problem. But if you face up to your problem and your anxiety, you generally can find some kind of solution.

A third false way of dealing with your anxiety is to rationalize it—that is, try to reason it away with some artificial or false explanation. You can blame somebody else, maybe your parents or your business partner or your spouse. But that just isn't good enough because, sooner or later, you have to accept your personal responsibility and meet it honestly. Most of us would like to think that our anxieties are caused by somebody else. It's easier on our own egos. But it doesn't work. We must learn to handle our own inner life before we can properly relate to other people. No matter who might have contributed to your problem, somewhere along the line you become responsible for the way you handle it.

There's a fourth false way of meeting anxiety, a way that so many people are taking these days. It is the way of drowning the anxiety with tranquilizers, alcohol, and narcotics. It has become an epidemic! Millions of people, young and old, are taking some easy way, some escape. Why are people alcoholics or drug addicts? Because they have anxieties they cannot handle. They can't stand it to be alone with their thoughts and their troubled conscience, and so they find some escape even if it destroys their lives and their homes. You know some such people by name. So do I. They glue their days together with barbiturates or sleeping pills or liquor, and they gradually destroy themselves because their real problem keeps getting worse.

Thank God there is a right and honest way to deal with anxiety and guilt. It is to open your heart and life to the love and grace of God through Christ. Something wonderful happens in your life when you receive God's boundless love. Maybe not all of your problems and anxieties will be permanently solved, but to open up your mind and heart to God's healing love is to come alive, to see all your problems in a different light. Some of us know this from experience.

Our text doesn't set before us an impossible ideal. It is practical and workable, but it must be constantly practised. Here it is again: "Have no anxiety about anything, but in everything by prayer and supplication with thanksgiving, let your requests be made known to God." Do that, live like that, and you won't need to run or escape or blame somebody else. You can live at peace with God and with yourself.

James Earl Massey
Christian Brotherhood Hour Speaker
1977-

Something of Value

"Are not five sparrows sold for two pennies? And not one of them is forgotten before God. Why, even the hairs of your head are all numbered. Fear not: you are of more value than many sparrows" (Luke 12:6-7).

"You are of . . . value." There are times when we are tempted not to believe this about ourselves, and sometimes other people act as if they don't believe this about us either. How often have you felt like nothing? Or, how often have you dared to judge another's worth? As a child growing up in the city I heard many names and epithets hurled in temper, things said to hurt and wound the hearer and making that person feel of no worth. I have seen the same thing happen among adults who certainly knew better than to act and speak that way. Not everybody will speak injuriously to others. Some persons maintain enough control to hold back certain thoughts, refusing to speak them because they know how unkind such speech would be. It is an old, old story: We know that a sense of personal value is hard-won, and it is not easily maintained in such a world. So we all favor those who treat us with respect. We all "like" those who by their treatment make us feel like a treasured friend. And how we avoid those persons who treat us otherwise. We recoil from anything that seems to threaten our sense of worth, be it a person or an unwanted experience. The text holds the word of Jesus to us, a word reminding us of our value when circumstances seem to deny that we count at all.

Like sparrows, *we too feel so small* in such a big and threatening world. So many things militate to make us feel so small. For instance, we want to look ahead to the future, but looking ahead is not easy. Events are proliferating in an entirely unpredictable fashion. So we are tempted to look back. But looking back is not safe because pausing too long in a backward look can only put us behind. While some futurists complain that improvements among us are not occurring as fast as they could and should, not keeping pace with our abilities, others among us lament that change is too much with us, and they are tempted to look suspiciously at anything new.

Which of us past thirty has not questioned the system that now surrounds us, a system that boasts a "new math," a "new English," indeed a "new learning"? Perhaps you too recall the magazine cartoon picturing two college coeds coming down the campus library steps. With their arms loaded down with books, one girl spoke lamentably to the other, "Every day there are more and more things to be ignorant about!" Our kind of world does stir within the feeling of being so small.

Certain kinds of living have played their sad part, also. With parents scrambling to get ahead, children are sometimes neglected, overlooked, and mistreated. Again and again I have counseled adults who were still hurting from childhood wounds from parental neglect or mistreatment. Most of those persons needed a healthy sense of self; they also held antagonistic feeling for one of the parents.

While waiting in a shopping center for my wife to complete her shopping list I browsed in the book department there. I chanced to overhear a young wife suggestively pleading with her husband: "Here is something you could give to your dad for Christmas." Her tone sounded so final and so weary, as if the couple had been searching now for some time. The husband drew near and examined the object she lifted to his view. Having heard her, I also turned, somewhat casually, and took a side long glance. The object was an excellently crafted model ship done in handcarved wood. The young man grabbingly reached for the price tag, then acted stunned as he blurted out, "Ugh! Thirty-five dollars!" Then with a scowl, he snapped, "But he's not worth *that much*!" I shuddered, wondering what that father had done to spoil the son's regard for him. I found myself wondering what price tag would have pleased him? How much is a father worth? How much is a son or a daughter worth? I finally concluded that that son had feelings against his father; he was hurting inside from something his father had or had not done toward him. Now, in his search for a cheap gift, he was betraying his own cheap view of his father's worth. That son did not feel valued, and so he was unwilling to confer value. If only he had known his worth in the sight of God! If only that young man could have forgiven his father! If he could find release from his feelings, that husband could be an agent of love to make his father sense his worth. Our text is for that son and ourselves. It is for all whom life has made feel so small—and even dared to act as less than we are. "You are of . . . value."

Like sparrows, *we too feel helpless* before the strong winds of life.

I looked out of our picture window one evening after an afternoon of storm winds in our city. Tree limbs were down here and there, and a few power lines were being repaired by city work crews. But I remember most the sight of a dead bird lying in the flower box beneath the window. The storm winds had been too strong for that bird to fight! Either that, or the clear plate glass had fooled the bird, appearing like a retreat into which it could fly for safety and rest. As I watched that scene of death I thought about our text.

There is stark realism in Matthew's parallel account of the text: "sparrows fall" (10:29—but not without the noticing eye of God. Sparrows alight and feed, always under God's careful attention; sparrows also fall, pushed or pulled by wind currents or by some calculating child with a slingshot or rifle.

That word *fall* is a world of pictured circumstances. Like sparrows, humans also fall, victims of life and living. This is the problem to which Jesus speaks. He reminds us that our worth is not diminished by tragedies, distresses, necessities.

Humans do fall: victims of hunger, poverty, wars, diseases, natural calamities, calculated cruelties. They fall victim to the sins of other people—and their own!

All of us have known and felt that deep-seated concern to stay alive, and we have experienced that equally painful ache for the courage to live. The taste for life is so often frustrated by the terrors of life. A noted scientist of our time was writing about this problem when he explained, "On certain days the world seems a terrifying thing: huge, blind and brutal. It buffets us about, drags us along, kills us with complete indifference . . . sweep(s) away in one moment what we had laboriously built up and beautified with all our intelligence and all our heart."[1] Sparrows fall. Humans fall. But our value is not diminished by the happening. Despite the experience, our value remains. "You are of . . . value."

Like sparrows, *we too seem so common* as to be of comparatively little worth. In Jesus' day, five sparrows could be bought for two pennies, and the more you bought the greater the discount. Volume decreased value, or so it seemed. But in God's sight it is not so.

Almost four billion persons people our world. Of what value can any one person be in the midst of so many? The New Testament word for *value* holds an insightful detail: it means to be differentiated, regarded as important because unique. It is true that humanity is of one common order, but there is a separateness and uniqueness of every person within that common order. Abraham Lincoln understood this and put it so well when he said, "God must have loved common people; He made so many of them." We might be stupified by the vast multitude around us in the world, and we might tend to miss the particularity of the persons we see in the mass, but God still deals with us individually, in "minute particulars," as William Blake explained it. Jesus was talking about the intimacy of God's dealings with us when he said, "Even the hairs of your head are all numbered. . . . You are of . . . value."

Jesus has spoken to us all. He knew that we humans wrestle with that painful uneasiness of mind called anxiety. Fully aware of our problem, that it is common to humankind, Jesus has spoken to reinforce our stand as we live in such a world. His words give us insight into God and ourselves. This text does not give us a systematic statement about life itself; it does not explain why life is as we find it, but it does give us a comforting and reassuring word about God and the help we are given as we live. Jesus has not tried to harmonize life as we know it with life as we wish it to be, but he has reminded us of our importance in the sight of God. Although we sometimes feel so little, so helpless, so common and undistinguished, that feeling is not the full or final fact about ourselves. We need not be ruined by emotional chaos caused by feelings of creaturehood. We are of value.

Dr. T. Franklin Miller tells of being on a ship at sea and having to miss his scheduled arrival time in Montreal because his ship went to the rescue of a man, deathly sick, on another ship about five hundred miles away. The ship bearing the sick man did not have a doctor or the surgical facilities needed to save his life. There was nervous excitement aboard the passenger liner as that ship hurried toward the stricken man. At the time of rendevous the sick man was transferred to the passenger vessel, and surgery was performed on him with successful results. The passenger liner docked at Montreal one day late, and nine hundred passengers were beset by complications with train, bus, and air travel connections. It was all because of *one man*—one man in need!

How did those passengers react to the forced change of plans? Dr. Miller talked with several of them during the hours of travel to reach the sick man. He was happily surprised that not one person with whom he talked had a single criticism about the rescue action. Personal inconveniences notwithstanding, every person seemed pleased that their ship could assist at such a time of need.[2] That reaction was more than a mere matter of being nice about the inevitable delay. There was a real concern to help because everybody knew that the sick man was a *person*. He had worth. He was someone. He had value.

Only God knows our value. God made us, so only God can fully measure our worth. But we get some understanding of how God values us when we look at what God has done in our interest through Jesus Christ. We are of such value in God's sight that Jesus died for us, "the righteous (One) for (us) the unrighteous, that he might bring us to God" (I Pet. 3:18). Only when we live in God's will is our worth focused, realized, and fulfilled.

[1] See Pierre Teilhard de Chardin, *The Divine Milieu* (New York: Harper and Brothers, 1960), p. 117; see also Christopher F. Mooney, *Teilhard de Chardin and the Mystery of Christ* (New York: Harper and Row, 1966), esp. pp. 13-33.

[2] See his editorial, "Rendevous in the North Atlantic," *Christian Leadership* magazine, October 1959, pp. 3, 20.

The Lord Is Good

"For the Lord is good; his steadfast love endures forever, and his faithfulness to all generations." (Ps. 100:5, RSV).

"The Lord is good." This is one of the strong lines the Hebrews would chant while at worship in the temple court. These words would resonate in the spirit of thanksgiving. Those who sang *knew* something; they were remembering how God had helped them. Their praise was loud but beautiful. "The Lord *is* good." Those who know this can well understand why the whole of this psalm is used with our standard Christian liturgy. Its words evoke praise and it is an excellent statement about *why* we praise God. The faithful rightly honor and serve God because, as our text strongly proclaims, God is faithful, loving, and good.

The Lord is a "good" God. Like faithful Israelites before us, we Christian believers have reason to witness about God's goodness. We too have discovered that in disposition and deeds the Lord God is for us. There is in God something prior and superior to us. There is in God a compassion that relates to our concerns, a helpfulness that relates to our hopes, a nearness that relates to our needs. God is good. We know this through God's dealings with us, and across the centuries those dealings have been manifold and individual. God is for us, and the evidences of God's good favor are so plentiful as to be "tasted," as it were, savored as a timely and well-prepared meal. That is how the psalmist put it when he wrote, "O taste and see that the Lord is good!" (Ps. 34:8). There has always been a compassion, helpfulness, and intimacy about the goodness of God to us. It is an expression of God's character. The psalmist wisely affirmed, "Thou art good and doest good" (119:68).

The compassions which bless us are traits of the Lord's goodness. The psalmist sang, "The Lord is good to all, and his compassion is over all that he has made" (145:9). Those compassions encompass our total lives, the entire range of our human experiences. But they supremely relate to our spiritual needs, especially the need to be forgiven for our sins. "For thou, O Lord, art good and forgiving," says Psalm 86:5, "abounding in steadfast love to all who call on thee."

Our foremost human problem in not learning how to shape our destiny, nor is it any supposed unequal wrestling match against fate. Our foremost human problem is clearing our sight to see the many evidences around us of the goodness and compassionate concern of God toward us. We need ears that can hear and eyes that can see.

God cares about us and wills our good, answering prayers beyond our deserving. God has made us free persons. God offers us wisdom, and assists us in our choices. God is for us. Yes, God commands but always for our good, and never coerces us against our will. Being good, God has set before us life and good, death and evil (Deut. 30:15). The choice is ours. The choice is always ours, because God is good and refuses to badger us into line. God relates to us all in love and seeks from us all a loving response.

The goodness of God is real. It is regular, and it reaches to all. God's is an unyielding and unrelenting goodness, steadfast despite any silly resistance on our part. Yes, there are times when God must in love chasten us, but because that is what we sometimes need it is good for us. God's relations with us might at times have to be austere, but they are never ambiguous. God is serious about our lives, sensitive to our needs, and works always to our good.

This was the understanding that sustained Joseph, whose experience of being rejected and sold into slavery by his jealous brothers could have soured his spirit against them. But Joseph, rescued and raised to high position by a concerned God, refused to seek revenge. Looking through the eyes of God, Joseph saw deeper into his brothers' dread deed than they. Their selfish deed had become God's opportunity. Grateful for God's goodness, Joseph refused to be the devil's agent. He reassured his fearful brothers, saying, "Fear not, for am I in the place of God? As for you, you meant evil against me; but God meant it for good, to bring it about that many people should be kept alive, as they are today. So do not fear; I will provide for you and your little ones" (Gen. 50:19-21). God had been good to Joseph, and so Joseph resolved to be good to his brothers who had wronged him.

"The Lord is good." We can affirm this even when our eyes are filled with tears and our hearts are filled with pain. True believers still celebrate God when the times are not good, when their efforts to do good are thwarted, making their experiences seem unrewarding. The praise of God must not be by psychological compulsion but should be a knowledgeable, thankful response. God's character has not changed when circumstances change or calamity occurs.

Yes, there are injustices in life. There are obstructions in our paths. There are frustrations in our experience and many inequities to ponder. Life as it is does raise heavy questions. There is the ugliness of sin and the inevitability of death. There are dark days in our minds and dark nights in our souls. There are sorrows, distresses, diseases, and stubbornly real evils in life. But even when life is not as we wish it, God is always as we need God to be—in goodness strengthening us to "keep on keeping on." The psalmist understood this and he confessed, "I believe that I shall see the goodness of the Lord in the land of the living" (27:13).

The Church's worship of God is not done as mere ceremonious behavior. The affirmations of the Church about God and Christ are not cold pious language, nor mere ancient and hallowed ritual. The true praise of God is in lively words,

104

words backed by experience, words like "the Lord is good."

Howard Thurman tells of an aged friend whose health began to fail. It has been her custom to begin each morning with a period of meditation. As she would open her eyes to life and her spirit to God she would always begin, "This is the day the Lord has made. I will rejoice and be glad in it." Upon going to bed at night she would change that line and say, "This is the night which the Lord has made. I will rest and relax in it." But she had a serious fall one day that left her shaken and in great pain. That night she lay in bed in great discomfort. As she turned out the light and prayed, she said, "This is the night which the Lord has made. I will relax and *cry* in it." As she thought about what she had just said, she found herself laughing a bit through her tears.[1] Yes, life had become harder to manage, but God was still witnessing to her spirit. Despite it all, she *knew* that God is good.

God has not left you without a witness in *your* life. God's goodness surrounds us all. "The Lord is good." To *know* this is to live for God, serving with dignity, thankfulness, and unfailing trust.

---

[1] Howard Thurman, *The Inward Journey* (New York and Evanston: Harper and Row, 1961), p. 132.

The Face of Jesus

"For it is the God who said, 'Let light shine out of darkness,' who has shone in our hearts to give the light of the knowledge of the glory of God in the face of Christ" (2 Cor. 4:6).

The text is part of a passage that tells the conspicuous importance of Jesus as the one who reveals God to us. Paul had referred to Moses as a man whose shining face betrayed his walk with God. A forty-day tryst with God on the mount had marked Moses as a special man among his people. A facial splendor lingered from their togetherness. It lingered so long that Moses kept his face veiled from the people. That veil hid the shocking glory. It also hid the sad fact that the splendor was steadily fading. Having the luster gave Moses honor; losing it humiliated him. Now, in the words of the text, Paul reflects upon the undimmed, unfading glory of the face of Jesus by which he had been illumined on the Damascus Road. A redeeming glory had captured Paul, bequeathing a true knowledge of God. The face of Jesus is revealing—and determinative. The text bids us to rehearse the significance of Jesus for faith and life.

So much can be said about the face of Jesus. I begin with this fact: Jesus had *a Semitic face*. Jesus of Nazareth was a Hebrew, a Semite from the line of Shem, one of the sons of Noah. This classification, together with the fact of where he lived, reminds us that he spoke one (or more) of the Semitic languages, evidently Palestinian-Aramaic and Hebrew. Now the Semites are not a race as such, but it is possible to say that an external appearance has tended to follow Hebrews, presenting us with a few features which we may call a Hebrew physiology.

Carlyle Marney tells of an old lady in Poland who was quite upset when she learned that Jesus had been a Jew, for she—provincial and uninformed—had never considered him as anyone but a Pole![1] One wonders what she afterward did with the new information; perhaps she decided to read her Bible with open eyes. Any proper theology of the New Testament, any proper historical approach to what is written there, demands our recognition of what Jesus was in the flesh. The Christian faith involves facts. And there is nothing more obvious in the New Testament than the fact that Jesus of Nazareth was a Hebrew, a Semite, with a face that physically reflected the lineage of which he was a part.

The face of Jesus was also *the face of a sufferer*. It is interesting that the portraitures of Jesus do not usually show this. In their attempts to portray the human Jesus, artists have evidently been led by other considerations, casting his countenance to reflect serenity, warmth, poise, and tenderness. Very few artists depict the feature of pensive suffering which must have been there facially because of his miseries as a poor and underprivileged Jew—not to mention his lot as a subjugated member of a minority group in a land tyrannized by Roman rule. Consider also that Jesus was constantly opposed in his work by religious bigots who held power. Jesus was a sufferer. Poor, harassed, sometimes helpless in the face of despots, Jesus of Nazareth knew the torments that etch lines into the human face—lines of concern, lines of resistance, lines of longing, lines of sorrow and suffering.

It is possible to trace this consideration about Jesus in the views of certain Church Fathers.[2] Influenced by the facts of his life, together with reflection on Isaiah 53:2-3, Justin Martyr, for instance, thought of Jesus as a man of frail body, weak, small in stature, and of a deprived countenance. The same reasoning appears in the thought of Clement of Alexandria, Origen, and a few others. But some other Church Fathers were impressed with the notion of a physically attractive Christ, and they searched the Old Testament for passages to support that concern. They found Psalm 45:2: "Thou are fairer than the children of men" (KJV), which they interpreted to show his gainly grace. So the ensuing centuries have brought us both sides of the question in the portraitures we view. The first-century believers who had seen Jesus in the flesh left us no portraits of his physical manhood, and the New Testament writings give us no word description of his facial cast. But the record of his poverty, his struggles, his disinheritedness, strongly suggests a countenance of serious cast, with lines of decisiveness by which to handle the falsities and contradictions that would have otherwise beset him. The face of Jesus was the face of a sufferer.

Jesus was a man of *set face*. I have spoken about lines of decisiveness on his face. There is an enlightening verse in Luke 9:51 about this: "When the days drew near for him to be received up, he set his face to go to Jerusalem." That expression "set his face" is a Semitic way of saying that Jesus firmed up his intention, strengthened his will, and bolstered his determination. He *had* to do so! There was so much calculated activity against Jesus as he did his work. Except for a calculated steadfastness Jesus could not have endured.

Jesus had to be a man of firm purpose and strong intention. It had to be so with him from the very first: from the time he deliberated in the wilderness weighing the issues of how he would serve, up to the time he struggled so resolutely in accepting the way of the cross. Jesus saw the masses of people abroad in the land. He saw a people needing a true leader, a people whose frenzied concern for freedom from Roman rule made them open prey to false messiahs. He saw them as sheep having no shepherd. The people he saw as he began his work were leaderless, vulnerable, and potentially dangerous because of their state of mind and affairs. He had to plan wisely for what he would say. He had to make precise calculations about their state of mind and affairs. He had to plan wisely for what he would say. He had to make precise calculations about their attitudes and plan with acuteness about what to dare and do.

Some issues he would only touch, and some others he would outrightly handle; he would discuss values in the light of Scripture, and he would press for scriptural solutions to problems. Jesus knew that a national uprising was possible, and that someone could take the command post by popular acclaim. He set himself against false routes to power, and that decision did not ever change.

Jesus was a man of set purpose. He was set against collaborating with the temple heirarchy. He was set against schemes linked with the landed gentry who were concerned about properties, prestige, and political security. He was set against unlawful practices and unfruitful attitudes. He rather set his life on the side of the Word of God, with strict intent to live out the insights of that Word within him. He set himself to be open with people, to risk himself in the interest of encounters in depth Jesus set himself to occasion direct contacts with the souls and needs of people, intent to reveal to them the very heart of God Set against moves prodded by fear and set for positive approaches to bad situations, Jesus was a man of personal imperative who knew himself to be on mission for God.

It must be said, then, that the face of Jesus was *the face of the Savior.* That is why he is hailed by us as the "Christ." Jesus reveals God to us, God in his saving role.

By now, you are aware that I have been speaking about the face of Jesus in a more than physical sense. When Paul wrote of "the glory of God in the face of Christ" he meant Jesus as a human figure, using "face" to denote the entire person. This is much like our way of speaking when we accuse someone of having had a "hand" in something; we mean that the person was part of an action.

One of the centralities of our faith is that the coming of Jesus has helped us to apprehend God historically and to have our personal history apprehended by God. God has revealed himself as saving person in Jesus.

The disciples of Jesus began to understand the dimensions of this fact as they lived with him. They later witnessed boldly to what they had discovered in his face because they found him to be one whose life had a special quality and whose person held a saving force. His life radiated the glory of God and bequeathed a sense of the very presence of the Lord God. The first witnesses gave their lives to the service of such a Christ. They were intent, under his Spirit, to help others apprehend God through their words, deeds, and Christ-illumined faces. Porphyry, longtime student under Plotinus, marveled at how that master's face grew radiant when he spoke of the deep things of God.[3] The first believers saw the light of God in the whole person of Jesus. He was for them a special person. It took them some time, however, before they finally realized that Jesus did not belong to just them but to all people.

The face of Jesus is the face of our Savior. It is the face of one who has loved us all enough to catch us up into his own life and meaning as the Son of God. It is his face that confronts us in our pride, our selfishness, our polarizations, or syncretism, our shortsightedness, our sin, and challenges us to live fully in the light of God's love and grace. We see in his face what it means to be a child of God.

My friend Dr. R. Eugene Sterner, longtime speaker on this Christian Brotherhood Hour, told some years ago of standing at the door of the sanctuary of the church he then pastored, greeting the parents as they were leaving the service. He picked up one little child and held him on one arm while greeting the child's parents. The little boy feelingly put his hand on the pastor's face, looked innocently into his eyes, and asked with all love in his query, "Are you Jesus?" Sterner trembled as he saw what his presence appeared to mean to an observing child. Any true Christian trembles upon realizing that his or her life will either reflect or obscure the claim Jesus makes upon us! There is only one Jesus, whose glory is undimmed, but having seen the light on his face, our lives must *reflect* that saving glory!

---

[1]Carlyle Marney, *Structures of Prejudice* (Nashville: Abingdon Press, 1961), p. 139.

[2]See the discussion of this controversy in Charles Guignebert, *Jesus* (New Hyde Park, N.Y.: University Books, Inc., 1956), esp. pp. 164-169. Trans. by S. H. Hooke.

[3]Cited by Rufus M. Jones, *Some Exponents of Mystical Religion (New York: Abingdon Press, 1930), see p. 53.*

The Christian Experience of the Holy Spirit

"So when they had come together, they asked him, 'Lord, will you at this time restore the kingdom to Israel?' He said to them, 'It is not for you to know times or seasons which the Father has fixed by his own authority. But you shall receive power when the Holy Spirit has come upon you; and you shall be my witnesses in Jerusalem and in all Judea and Samaria and to the end of the earth' " (Acts 1:6-8, RSV).

Before his ascension, Jesus reminded and reassured his disciples about his earlier promise to give them power.

These disciples thought at first that Jesus' promise about power meant political and national supremacy for Israel. They could readily envision a restored autonomy for their nation, full freedom from Rome for their people. These men were itching to break the yoke of Rome from the nation's neck, redeem Israel, and fulfill the nation's hopes. These concerns were seething in their subconscious minds when Jesus mentioned again "the promise of the Father" (Acts 1:4) and being "clothed with power from on high" (Luke 24:49). So they put the question to Jesus, eager for his word to confirm their strong expectation: "Lord, will you at this time restore the kingdom to Israel?" (v. 6). Jesus parried that question wisely; he knew that time and experience would answer them properly. They would soon learn that his promise about power involved abilities and happenings of a different kind, that their lives would serve a higher end than political uses and national concerns. The power Jesus promised to his followers would be known in their experience of the Holy Spirit. The Book of Acts shows us this in vivid detail.

According to the Book of Acts, the Christian experience of the Holy Spirit is one of *realized presence*. Being ''filled with the Holy Spirit'' (2:4) means a conspicuous relation with God; it means an understood share in God's will. It includes an awareness of relationship and being engaged by God.

The biblical doctrine of the Holy Spirit is one of the richest sets of teachings found in Scripture. This doctrine is not a mere leftover from the Jewish background of the first Christians. The biblical doctrine of the Holy Spirit is an emphatic statement about how God shares with us inwardly. It tells us about how God penetrates our lives by his presence, participating with us in the details and drama of living. The doctrine about the Holy Spirit contains deep truths about an essential matter: how God interacts with our human spirit, sharing mind, character, guidance, love, and a helping hand. One noted theologian once traced all the biblical references to the Holy Spirit and summed them up within two expressions: God-at-hand, *intimacy,* and God-at-work, *potency*.[1]

Jesus spoke often about the Holy Spirit, and he placed the accent on the relation between the Holy Spirit and himself. Jesus explained his service as directly related to the help of the Holy Spirit, saying, ''The Spirit of the Lord is upon me'' (Luke 4:18). The Christian's experience of the Holy Spirit is also one of understood help through divine presence mediated within us by God's own Spirit.

The Christian experiences the Holy Spirit as the one who *adjusts personality*. The Holy Spirit specializes in focusing personality. The Spirit is expert in drawing tight the otherwise loose strings of personal life, holding them with the sure grip of grace and godliness. And what is the model of adjustment? Jesus Christ. The Holy Spirit works within us to make us like Jesus: like him in mind, like him in will, like him in character, in disposition, in obedience, in faith, in service, in love.

112

Irenaeus had this in mind when he said that the Holy Spirit "adjusts us to God."[2]

The noblest work of the Holy Spirit is the shaping of Christlike persons. The Spirit, therefore, works for continual adjustments, helping us toward a focused identity as decided Christians. By the Spirit's help we learn and live holiness. The Holy Spirit helps us with our instincts, our urges, our feelings, our thoughts, our reactions and works within our memories, helping us to handle the history of our sad and sinful past and properly shape the history made available to us in Christ. The Holy Spirit helps us to focus our intention, strengthen our will, firm up our determination, and live with openness to the will of God. The Spirit helps us handle the demands of each new day and deepens our hope when life seems forbidding and our experiences appear dead end. The Spirit takes us beyond the limitations we see in ourselves. That is why the Holy Spirit "fills" and "possesses" us. The writer was correct who explained, "Human personality is so constructed that it must be possessed if it is to escape the prison of self-possession."[3] The high distinctiveness of being Christian is that one has been mastered, possessed, caught up in the will of God by the Spirit. The Holy Spirit makes us productive in right living and keeps us focused for God's use.

The Christian's experience of the Holy Spirit keeps one *sensitive to need.* The preaching seen in the Book of Acts must be so understood. It was truthful preaching done with human need in mind; thus Peter and John and the others refused to stop preaching the truth about Christ even when threatened by unbelieving Jewish authorities. They continued to minister despite accusations, despite wrong labels "pinned" on them, malicious stories told against them, and repeated efforts of inflamed enemies to harrass and disrupt their work. The Holy Spirit helped them to deal with human needs, helped them in their prayers, their planning, their caring, their resourcefulness, their boldness, their patience, their persistence, and in their clear message.

The many healings attributed to the hands of the apostles must be traced to the work of the Holy Spirit in them. The healings helped distressed bodies and minds. Those healings also honored Christ; they were evidences of his continuing ministry of care.

The Christian's experience of the Holy Spirit makes one ready for *positive witnessing about Christ*. The Book of Acts lets us see the many activities in which the early church was involved. Primary among all the activities was witnessing about Jesus, speaking out about his life and work. The Christians we see active there did not choose between talk and deeds; they knew that both are necessary and they kept them in balance. Those Christians did not flaunt labels, they busied themselves expressing outwardly what they valued within. Those Christians were not preoccupied with positions but were concerned rather about assignments understood and fulfilled. Not all of them were highly educated, but all were knowledgeable about Jesus and they witnessed about what they knew. They did not speak out of their doubts but out of their faith. Like us, they probably had many theories but they witnessed rather about their experiences.

The Book of Acts is filled with instances of positive witnessing. And those records show what happened when witnessing was done in the power of the Spirit. We must never forget that the power Jesus promised his people was linked to the work of being witnesses: "But you shall receive power when the Holy Spirit has come upon you; and you shall be my witnesses in Jerusalem and in all Judea and Samaria and to the end of the earth" (1:8). The ministry of the Holy Spirit in our lives is especially related to the work of witnessing about Christ, even helping us with courage to die for him.

The Christian's experience of the Holy Spirit generates within us *a higher patriotism*. Men and women filled with the Holy Spirit can get beyond limiting selfishness and clasp hands in unity for common life and cooperative work. Under the help of the Holy Spirit, prides yield and the struggle for positions ends. Those who are trained by the Spirit learn to view themselves as sharers, as a community, as a family in God. Those who receive the Holy Spirit are under charge forever to make common cause with each other. Acts speaks of this as being in "one accord" (2:1, KJV).

The first disciples had to learn this under the daily help of the Holy Spirit. That group of Jews at first felt more determined by issues of the day than by eternal concerns. But once those believers were filled with the Spirit, their lesser concerns fell into proper place; their lower patriotism yielded to the power of a higher one. It was not long before Peter and the others realized that they were but one part of a new world family, part of the beginning of a new people, and their lives opened increasingly to accept and regard non-Jews in the Christian faith. A new attitude possessed them, making it possible for non-Jewish believers like Cornelius (Chap. 10) and Simeon Niger (Chap. 13) to feel at home in their midst.

A true Christian belongs to more than some nation and locale; he or she belongs mainly to a risen Lord. Stronger ties than class or race bless our lives. A higher life claims us as its agents. A richer set of experiences flavors our living.

Let me summarize what I have said about the Christian experience of the Holy Spirit. It is one of realized presence. It is an experience of having the personality adjusted. It is an experience of sensitivity to human need in the name of Christ. It is an experience that prods positive witnessing about Christ. It is one of a higher patriotism and personal loyalty. All of these features, plus many more, make up the Christian's experience of the Holy Spirit. And that experience is open to all: "For the promise is to you and to your children and to all that are far off, every one whom the Lord our God calls to him" (Acts 2:39).

[1] Henry Pitney Van Deusen, *Spirit, Son and Father* (New York: Charles Scribner's Sons, 1958), pp. 18, 26.

[2] Quoted by F. W. Dillistone, *The Holy Spirit in the Life of Today* (London: The Canterbury Press, 1946), see p. 10.

[3] Reinhold Niebuhr, *The Nature and Destiny of Man* (London: Nisbet and Co., Ltd., 1943), vol. 2, p. 116.

Let the Church Be the Church!

The church at Corinth was in trouble. Unwise and ungodly happenings there had undermined the effectiveness of that congregation. Spiritual life there was being choked off by selfishness, and the beauty of Christian standards was being marred by sin. Paul's first letter to that church lets us know plainly that some members there were living as if they had never been redeemed; their deeds were not just questionable, but downright wrong. Those deeds were self-defeating, and they were open obstacles to the integrity and true meaning of the Church. Paul sought to correct the situation, and so he sent the members these words: "I wrote to you not to associate with anyone who bears the name of brother if he is guilty of immorality or greed, or is an idolater, reviler, drunkard, or robber—not even to eat with such a one" (1 Cor. 5:11). And then, aware that some who were guilty of such sins would not readily stop their doings, Paul quoted a pointed refrain from Deuteronomy, challenging all who meant business for God, " 'Drive out the wicked person from among you' " (1 Cor. 5:13. See Deut. 17:7).

This was strong and forceful language! But the situation at Corinth demanded it. The church there needed to be the Church. The members there needed to live up to what God expected of them.

It is always a sad state of affairs when divine standards are not honored by those who profess to be the Lord's people. Paul was especially indignant about the spiritual problems at Corinth. He refused to be silent and let things run their course. He spoke up by letter and rebuked that one who had married his own stepmother, a woman who had been the wife of his father. Common sense should have advised him against this. Paul called the selfish man a wicked person, and he rebuked the congregation for letting that kind of thing happen without a clear word of judgment spoken against it.

It makes one wonder where the moral judgment of the church stood before Paul volunteered to deal with the case. It makes one wonder also whether the offending person was too prominent a member to be censured. Did that man hold some position in the church that influenced other members to be lenient toward him? It seems that the church was divided over the issue. But why?

What was behind such happenings at Corinth? The conditions there were sad, and Paul wrote to correct them. Alert to the emotional depth of these matters, he gave a strong and uncompromising verdict: "Put the wicked ones out! Hold a meeting, settle the issues—expel the wrongdoers!"

There are times when a congregation needs to discipline some of its members. There are times when those who defy clear moral teaching must be expelled from the fellowship.

There have always been standards to govern the Lord's people. The church remains the Church when its members obey the Lord. The Church was given standards to follow, and all who belong to it are expected to live by them. The Corinthian letters of Paul make this abundantly clear. When he addressed the congregation at Corinth as "the church of God" and referred to the members as persons "called to be saints" (1 Cor. 1:2), Paul was reminding his readers about the high order of Christian discipleship. He was setting a moral tone for the message he was about to share more fully. He was intent to make his readers think clearly about the Church and help them live fully as God's people.

Some time ago a magazine to which I subscribe carried on its cover a photograph of the late Arturo Toscanini, the famed orchestral conductor. The photograph had appeared so often in so many publications that the editors hastened to explain why that same photograph was being used again. The editors wrote, "Nearly every photograph of Toscanini conducting has been published many times; this one is no exception—but it remains a beautiful picture."[1] The standards of the Church have been stated and heard again and again, but they still present a beautiful picture. Every standard our Lord gave is a thing of beauty and blessing. Beautiful standards, faithfully honored and ardently lived, keep the Church beautiful and contagious.

The Church was not intended to be like the world but to change the world. It is no place for those who want to persist in sin, the Church is for those who are tired of sin and are resisting it. All those who truly want to follow Christ must accept his way of living. No other way can please God. If you *claim* to be a Christian, then *be* one. Live by sound standards. Let your behavior match your testimony. And insist that your local church do the same.

There are distinct differences between the true Church and the wayward world, between those who are godly and those who resist his will. Paul had those clear differences in mind when he rebuked those members who were not living as they should. When Paul told the church to expel unrepentant offenders, he was within his rights. Those persons were steadily violating the purpose and standards of the Church. Paul's jurisdiction as an apostle of the Lord gave him authority to set things in order. So he pronounced judgment in the name of the Lord Jesus. The church there needed to be the Church, and so certain offenders were to be removed from membership. They were to be regarded no longer as brothers or sisters in the faith. How else could the church remain the Church?

The Church is something other than a statistical list of nice persons. It is something other than a promotional enterprise generated within a congenial setting of friends. It is something other than a community betterment agency. The Church Jesus formed is a fellowship of faith and godly behavior. Its members are the redeemed: they are persons whose lives have been changed by grace and whose concern is to please God and share God's love with others. This is how the New Testament describes the Church. No local congregation can be part of *that* Church unless its members relate fully to its Savior and Lord.

Paul wrote to remind the Corinthian believers about this. He knew that the congregation needed renewal. He wrote to help its members repent, be renewed, and be the Church.

The history of the Church has been a history of reform and renewal. The Church lives and works in the world where ideas, trends, and forces threaten its life and movement. The late Charles Ewing Brown once wrote,

> The Church of God on earth, the spiritual community of believers continuing through all history, . . . is quite lacking in the gift of omniscience and others of the infinite qualities of God. Under these circumstances, laboring as we do under the historic limitations of man's finitude . . . we have no reason to assert that the . . . community . . . would be preserved from all error and thus freed from any necessity of reformation.
>
> "We might, in fact, say boldly that the true spiritual community, consisting as it does of fallible human beings, would often require to be checked on an erroneous course and led back time and again to the original standards of Christian doctrine and practice. The mere assertion that the church is composed of masses of finite human beings is sufficient justification for the repeated calls to reformation through the ages."[2]

Our finitude, misused freedom, and failure: these are the three human realities against which the Church must forever brace itself. These are why clear teaching and inward renewal are always necessary to help the church be the Church.

Reform always happens because someone becomes concerned—concerned enough to pray about the problem and then act to solve it. That prayerful, concerned, and active person brings truth to bear upon the problem—truth that yields a ready and imperative vision.

Here is the usual pattern: something unworthy happens in a church; then something happens within the heart of someone who becomes concerned about the unworthiness; then practical action is taken and a possible reform is on the way.

Reformers are always prepared in the cross fire between truth and tragic circumstances, and true reformers always take their side with truth. They do not wait for any organizational permission before they act. No organization gives them their strength. God gives it, and God helps them to take their stand, speak their word, and do their deed.

When finitude blinds us, when freedom is misused, when failure results, reformers are needed. And they come, with sound teaching to be heard and regarded if repentance and renewal are to happen where they should.

A person can err. A congregation can err. Reformers and clear standards help us to detect such error and correct ourselves. Those who are serious about God and grace will obey the reforming word.

Paul worked to reform the church at Corinth and set it on the right path again. He spoke the needed word of rebuke and called for the needed adjustments. He defined the points of failure and defied all evil that opposed him. He was intent to help that church be the Church.

Being the Church means a firm standing in Christ. It means standing out from the world. It means committed living on the part of all who claim to belong. Now as then, the church needs to be the Church.

---

[1]*High Fidelity* magazine, March 1957 issue, p. 3.

[2]*When Souls Awaken:* An Interpretation of Radical Christianity (Anderson Ind.: Gospel Trumpet Co., 1954), pp. 20-21.

God Wants You Saved!

God our Savior . . . desires all men to be saved and to come to the knowledge of the truth'' (1 Tim. 2:3-4).

The great passion of God is to save humanity. God "desires all men to be saved," and that desire includes *you*.

Salvation is the basic message of the Bible. It is the central teaching to which its pages give witness. Salvation is the purpose behind the coming of Jesus to our world. Coming as the one for all, Jesus did his atoning work once for all. Paul was pointing to this when he wrote: "For there is one God, and there is one mediator between God and men, the man Christ Jesus, who gave himself as a ranson for all . . ." (vv. 5-6).

God wants to save us all! All of God's ways of dealing with us are especially concerned about one result: our salvation.

Salvation is the great human need. It is our primary and our ultimate need.

Every human being needs the benefits of salvation. We humans need to be delivered from a life of sin. We need to be rescued from the enslaving power of evil. We need to be released from condemning guilt. We need forgiveness for the sins we have committed against God and each other. Salvation grants all of this. It means forgiveness for sins. It gives release from guilt. It removes our condemnation. It frees us from the tyranny of sin and delivers us from the wrath of God against disobedience.

Salvation is also inward healing of the soul, the curing of what sin has left diseased. Salvation is inward newness, a fresh start, inward peace, wholeness, well-being. To be saved is to be put into right relationship with God. It is to be readied for life, death, and the hereafter.

Surely you will agree that we humans need these benefits, that we need to be saved. This need demands top priority treatment. God has given this need passionate attention. The Bible reports God's planning and action to save us. "God our Savior . . . desires all men to be saved and to come to the knowledge of the truth." "All men" includes you. God wants you saved.

We cannot save ourselves. God must save us. The text refers to "God, our Savior."

God initiated the planning and action to save us. God has acted graciously toward us all despite our sinful failures and stubborn rebellion. Although we resisted God's will, broke divine laws, and spurned divine love, God has lovingly continued to claim us as children.

God is eager to show concern for us. God wants to rescue us from the grip and ruin of sin. God wants to forgive and renew us. God wants to save us, preparing us for history and eternity.

Have you let God save you yet? Have you let God begin in you that process that makes your life become what it needs to be? God wants to save you, and will save you if you allow it. God will handle your sinful past, guide you through the maze of the present, and give you a future shaped by his wisdom and love.

Please note that "God . . . *desires* all men to be saved." That does not mean that God has decreed all people shall be saved. It means that all people who so desire to be saved, can be saved. The provision has been made. Our responsibility is to accept what God has offered.

Salvation happens when we desire what God desires, when we desire for ourselves what God desires for us and act on God's provision to obtain it. God laid the plans for our salvation. That was God's sovereign and gracious deed. We must accept the plan and act on it. That is our freedom and the

way to accept grace.
must accept the plan and act on it. That is our freedom, and the way to accept grace.

God is eager to see us all enjoy salvation and escape lostness. We are to "come to the knowledge of the truth" and live as redeemed persons. Until that happens to a man or woman, he or she is in a lost condition.

There is a real distinction made in the New Testament between being lost and being saved. This difference is not figurative, it is real. It is a difference that should stir us to great seriousness and an active faith. Let there be no confusion about this: Just as there is a salvation, there is a lostness, and the distinction between being saved and being lost must not be forgotten, slightly regarded, neglected, nor debunked except to our ruin. Salvation is the great human need. It relates not only to history but to eternity.

God wants all people to be saved because God loves us and seeks our good. But we must desire salvation and must freely choose it because God will not force salvation upon us.

Salvation is God's greatest gift for us. It is a most practical gift because it suits our greatest need. God is mindful of our total human concerns and needs and has acted in providence and grace to bless us in all areas of our living. But God is supremely concerned about our spiritual welfare. To receive everything else from God's hands and not take salvation as well is to miss God's greatest benefit and leave our greatest need unmet. God wants you saved!

Have no misgivings—you can be saved. You will be saved. All who come to God seeking forgiveness and favor will be saved. That is God's promise. That is your hope. That can be your experience now.

As you come to God there is one who speaks on your behalf. That one is Jesus Christ, the Son of God. He is the mediator, the go-between, the one "who gave himself as a ransom for all." He identifies with you as you come, and because of his saving deed on the cross you can claim from God all that salvation was meant to be.

You can claim the present benefits of being saved:

reconciliation with God and release from the power and the penalty of sin. You can also trust God for what must come in the future, namely the redemption of your body after death and the glorious benefits of the life to come. The ministry of Jesus has made all of this possible for us. God wants you to have a share in it. God wants you saved!

The sharing begins when you repent of your sins, calling upon God to be forgiven and renewed. This decision is basic. A definite break with sin is demanded, and a decisive trust in Christ is required. Salvation is more than a doctrine to be believed; it is a life to be lived. It is more than a principle; it is fact. It is not our achievement. It is a gift, a ready gift to those who accept God's Son.

Have you ever turned to God and asked to be saved? Do you have the assurance that salvation has happened in your life? Are the fruits of that experience evident in your daily life? If you are saved, then let nothing hinder your progress in faith, hope, love, and behavior.

If you have never sought the Lord—or have turned *from* him to resume a selfish walk in sin, then I speak now to call you in his name. God wants you saved. You need to be saved. God is ready to save you if you are willing and ready to let it happen.

They Thought He Was Mad

"And when his family heard it, they went out to seize him, for people were saying, 'He is beside himself' " (Mark 3:21, RSV).

Persons truly committed to the will of God are sometimes thought to be too serious. They are sometimes ridiculed as "beside themselves." Sometimes their critics think of them as mentally disturbed, or even as mad. The text reports an instance when Jesus was charged with having lost his mind. When Jesus' mother, brothers, and close friends heard what some leaders were saying about him and against him, they agreed to try to persuade him that it was time to go home. These friends and family members were anxious for his safety and sanity.

The fears within a family for its members can be many and long-lived. Many of us have trembled in fear, filled with anxiety as we watched some illness sapping the strength of a loved one. The fear that they might die did not let us rest easily. Many of us have been apprehensive about our parents as they added more years to their dwindling strength. Their feebleness stirred deep concerns within us and wrung strong prayers from us on their behalf.

But there is nothing quite like a parents' fears for their children. There is a natural concern to be with the children as they grow up and go out into life, and there are steady prayers to God that the children will remain well in body and sound in mind.

Jesus' loved ones were anxious about him. He was saying things that were different. Although he was a popular speaker with the crowds, the religious authorities did not sanction his words or his work. Reports were circulating about his special powers. He even claimed to hear voices and to have seen visions. But he did not seem to be caring for himself. He was always with crowds. Perhaps he was beginning to feel too important? Maybe his popularity was becoming too burdensome? With all of the conflict mounting against him his family became increasingly disturbed. They therefore came to take Jesus away from the crowd. They thought that he needed time to come to himself and find his way again.

But such fears on their part were ill-founded. They had grossly misjudged Jesus. Jesus was not mad. Zeal for God is not madness; it is the sanity that shows up the madness of others.

The Apostle Paul was not mad when he was charged as being beside himself. Acts 26:24 tells us that Portius Festus made that charge against Paul as the Apostle was on trial before him. Having learned about Paul's excellent background, Festus suggested that his great learning had affected him. This might have been his attempt to deal kindly with Paul since the debate was a severe one involving Paul and the Sanhedrin. Or maybe Festus said this to gain some time in handling Paul's case. He had just taken over as procurator in Caesarea and was inexperienced in handling Jewish matters. Paul was not sure just how Festus might decide the case, and so he appealed to be tried in Rome at Caesar's court.

Paul was not mad. He was just eager to make everyone else a Christian. He wanted to win the world for Christ. Like Jesus his Lord, Paul lived to do God's bidding.

Hostile critics often speak against agressive believers as "too serious." Those who fear being influenced by ardent witnesses try to protect themselves by claiming that the witnesses are mentally disorganized. But stinging words of truth cannot be dismissed by being labeled as silly or absurd notions. One might, as the saying goes, "Give a dog a bad name, and kill it," but statements of truth cannot be so dismissed. Nor can the contagious spirit of a person who is "out-and-out" for God.

There was in Jesus a fundamental goodness. He was open in his dealings and caring in his attitudes. People felt something when Jesus was around, especially when he taught and preached. There was something basic in his words. Whatever he did had contagion. All of this made his critics feel limited, inept, and even unclean.

Jesus was not self-centered. Jesus was not narrow. He had a power for good—and he used it doing good. People trusted him. Crowds followed him. His critics could not understand his appeal and they questioned his integrity. They plotted against his safety and stirred some to question his sanity.

When Jesus' family and friends got wind of this they wanted to get Jesus home, out of the crowd. "They went out to seize him, for they said 'He is beside himself.' " Not so. Jesus was a sane man on business for a saving God

Some critics accused Martin Luther of being "beside himself" as he went about his work. Some still cannot believe that God was in Luther's work. They see his attempts to reform the church as divisive, and instead of seeing him as a reformer they call him a revolutionist. But God did use Martin Luther and his colleagues, and together they recovered a lot of lost ground biblically.

The Church at large is greatly indebted to such reformers for their insight, courage, and persistent work. The church needed a clear doctrinal statement about salvation, and Luther gave it from his study of the Bible. Something of lasting significance is always accomplished for the Church when we return to Scripture as our sourcebook for faith and doctrine. True freedom comes through the truth. If taking Scripture seriously is madness, then the world needs more of it.

But is is not madness to give one's life to the study and handling of truth. It is not madness to live by a vision God has given through the Bible to the world. It is not madness to believe in God, love him, and seek always to please him. It is not madness to honor biblical values and obey biblical norms for behavior. It is not madness to accept the lordship of Christ. It is madness to resist that lordship and try to live on one's own as if there were no God and no accountability.

It is not madness to trust what Jesus taught about life and death, good and evil, heaven and hell, time and eternity. If ever anyone knew the truth about these, Jesus did. It is madness to question his teachings and trust one's own mind to find meaning.

Where was sanity when morality was scrapped by some in honor of situational ethics? Where was sanity when the distinctions between good and evil were lost and a new generation grew up in our world with no sense of accountability to God, family, or society? Where was plain common sense when the so-called new morality made personal preference and circumstances the new absolutes? Yes, some persons caught in that trap were sincere, but that sincerity cannot rescue them from the confusion that has ensnared their minds and lives. The so-called new thoughts are the old evils. Some things cannot be rightly known or understood without hearing from God's Word about them. Some issues cannot be rightly resolved without calling upon principles, morals, rules.

Monstrous errors afflict our society and world. Grievous mistakes fill the pages of history and plague our lives. Deep guilt saturates the mind of this generation. That guilt is something more than a neurotic symptom. It is a reminder that God has not left us without a witness. So many persons have tried to shout that witness down and drown it out with all kinds of modern noise and activities. But life still calls for the right absolutes. We still need landmarks to know where were are.

Sanity will return when morals make a comeback. And who can teach us more about morals than Jesus? Who but Jesus can make us wise for salvation?

George Whitefield was mightily used of God in the Great Awakening. Some of his critics accused him of being "beside himself." And why? Because of his "mad step" of daring to preach to the masses in the open air. Burdened for souls, Whitefield moved his ministry out from the church buildings and into the streets. Insensitive church leaders criticized him for doing so.[1] They thought he was mad.

Whitefield was not mad except to those who were ignorantly tied into one system, those who associated salvation with the cold walls of a church building and the worship services conducted there.

The thought of taking the preaching outside conjured fears in Whitefield's critics. But Whitefield did not fear what they feared, nor did he regard what they regarded. The critics feared street riots. True, the populace was an uneasy bunch. The Lower Moorlands was not the place of guaranteed order, and some of those who gathered along the streets were sometimes rowdy—a rabble, if ever there was one. But Whitefield wanted to carry the gospel to them too, and so he dared to preach to street sellers, hawkers, agitators, thieves, and arsonists. He dared because he desired to do so. Mad? No! Just a man on business for God. Just an obedient man forgetting himself in God's work. Whitefield explained himself in the words of Luke 4:18, "(God) hath anointed me to preach the gospel to the poor" (KJV).

Jesus gave himself to his work. He forgot himself in the will of God. The Christian faith calls us all into self-forgetting. Paul knew this and called it to the attention of the Corinthians. Said he, "For if we are beside ourselves, it is for God; if we are in our right mind, it is for you" (2 Cor. 5:13). Then he added, "For the love of Christ controls us . . . that those who live might live no longer for themselves but for him who for their sake died and was raised" (vv. 14, 15).

Christian life at its best is a self-forgetting commitment to God and God's service. Such a commitment does "make waves" as we move in a world that feels threatened by our values and major concerns. The contrast between what the world honors and what Christ calls us to be and do does cause tension; it does make Christians appear somewhat strange, and, yes, perhaps "mad." But the love of Christ controls us: his love for us, and our love for him which he inspires.

A world-famous concert pianist once advised some piano students that artistic excellence demands everlasting practice, extraordinary persistence, unfailing discipline, and the heart to let music always come first in their lives. Then she added,

"Music also needs a little madness. If you aren't a little mad, you will never (succeed in) this life."[2] It will take nothing less to claim our world for God.

[1] See John Pollock, *George Whitefield and the Great Awakening* (Garden City, NY: Doubleday and Co., Inc., 1972), esp. pp. 97-107.

[2] Gina Bachauer, From an interview with Dean Elder, *Clavier* magazine, March 1970.

Stress Can Be Useful

"For we do not want you to be ignorant, brethren, of the affliction we experienced in Asia; for we were so utterly, unbearably crushed that we despaired of life itself. Why, we felt that we had received the sentence of death; but that was to make us rely not on ourselves but on God who raises the dead; he delivered us from so deadly a peril, and he will deliver us; on him we have set our hope that he will deliver us again" (2 Cor. 1:8-10, RSV).

One word can be written over the life of the Apostle Paul: that word is *stressful*. But two more words should be added to it: *stressful—but productive*. Paul was productive because he learned how to use stress and make it serve him.

We could all write the word *stressful* over our lives, too. But we too can learn how to use stress and made our lives productive. My textural passage deals with this. It is a statement from Paul, who wrote to the Corinthian believers, "For we do not want you to be ignorant, brethren, of the affliction we experienced in Asia; for we were so utterly, unbearable crushed that we despaired of life itself. Why, we felt that we had received the sentence of death; but that was to make us rely not on ourselves but on God who raises the dead; he delivered us from so deadly a peril, and he will deliver us; on him we have set our hope that he will deliver us again" (2 Cor. 1:8-10).

Something had happened in the Apostle's life that made him know he was in extreme external danger. Paul confessed that he felt depressed. His words reflect that depression: "utterly, unbearably crushed." He thought that death was imminent, and that no escape was possible this time. We do not know whether Paul had suffered a severe illness or was again the victim of death-dealing hostility against him. We do know that whatever happened was nearly fatal to Paul's life and work and it caused him to "despair of life itself." That deadly peril affected Paul's hopes. Being delivered deepened his faith. The deliverance was so timely, so miraculous, and so appreciated that Paul viewed it as a kind of resurrection. Paul had faced stressful times before—even calculated dangers against his life—but he felt still closer to God this time. He now realized in his own experience that God indeed "raises the dead."

Some occasions of stress are like a death. They do make us feel "utterly, unbearably crushed." Life can sometimes press us so heavily that we despair of living. We lose our zest, our energy levels fall, unhappiness swamps us, and anxiety mounts high in mind and spirit. Most of us have known such times of felt inadequacy. Those are the times we feel the need for God, and we feel that need at the deepest levels of our being. Those are the times we realize that we cannot rely on ourselves "but on God who raises the dead."

The word *stress* comes to us from the world of physics and engineering. It originally meant *strain*. The picture is of some force being exerted upon something to test its powers to hold up under pressure and remain what it was made to be and do. Brought over into common life, the word *stress* is now used to describe the pressures we experience. It represents all that makes it difficult to achieve our plans with ease. It stands for everything which tests our strength to endure, making us feel the need for help in handling it.

The whole experience of being under stress makes us question what is happening to us. It's more than a felt experience. Stress forces us to deal with our feelings about it all, and we need faith to see beyond it all and handle ourselves wisely under the pressure.

Some kinds of stress can produce damage in us, but not all stress has to be damaging. There is no way to avoid or escape some stress, but there is a way to view it, and there is a way we can put it to use and make it serve our lives.

Stress is useful when it makes us exercise our faith, when it makes us stretch our souls and develop spiritual muscle.

One of the greatest secrets of enduring life is to know that outside forces need not control us. Our lives were meant to be controlled from within by a sound interpretation of who we are, and what we mean to God, others, and ourselves. It is when this inner control falters that stress does its great damage in us. But as long as faith informs us, we can grow stronger and stronger by wrestling with what is happening to us.

Struggle strengthens us. Physical activity blesses the body, and spiritual activity strengthens the soul.

More and more reports have been appearing about the importance of regular work and exercise for the body and mind. We are being told more and more that work, even hard work, is good for us, while too much rest can be quite damaging in the long run. Normal work does not usually harm healthy tissues of the body; it rather develops and extends the range of our physical abilities. But too much rest can be damaging. It affects blood circulation and causes the muscles to lose their tone. Perhaps you too have noticed that your appetite tends to slacken when you do not work or exercise properly. Interestingly, doctors are careful about advising bed rest except at acute stages of illness.

Now just as the body is blessed and served by the stress and strain which call out the best in it, so are our souls helped when put under pressures that make us stretch ourselves in faith and hope. Paul was referring to this when he wrote, "For the sake of Christ, then, I am content with weaknesses, insults, hardships, persecutions, and calamities; for when I am weak, then I am strong" (2 Cor. 12:10). He viewed his stressful experiences as exercises for his soul.

Paul also knew that stress could help deepen him in godliness.

Our moral life is strengthened whenever we successfully handle stress, especially the stress of some temptation. Whenever our decision to live for God is tested by evil we have an occasion when godliness can become more deeply engrained in us. Every time of testing is integral to our moral growth.

There is a sense in which we help to shape the pattern of our lives. We have a share in determining the direction of our moral growth. We become what we decide. It happens as we live under stress and trust God to make it all "work for good with those who love him, who are called according to his purpose" (Rom. 8:28). God stands ready to help us become what we see in Jesus, the Son of God, who matured as he "learned obedience through what he suffered" (Heb. 5:8).

Moral steadfastness results when stress is rightly handled. Jesus is supreme proof of this. And stress helped Paul to deepen in godliness. Paul determined that his times of stress would work to the spiritual good in his life.

The experience of stress should keep us reminded that we are still in process, that we are on pilgrimage in God's will.

Wayne E. Oates once commented that "Christian development is not a smoothly contoured ascent from one stage to another. Nor is it ever completed and finished," at least not here in this kind of world. We are in process. We are learning as we live, struggling as we go, but edging closer to our goal with each passing day. Stress is important to that process.

Douglas V. Steere recalls an experience that helps us to grasp the meaning of this statement more aptly. He and his wife were in Holland, walking along a street where a noted church building stood. While passing they noticed the high flight of stone steps, about thirty-five or forty in all, leading up to the church door from the street below. A child about three years old had climbed those steps and was standing at the top. He was full of glee over his accomplishment and was calling back down in happiness to his watching parents. Steere and his wife continued to watch and soon saw that the child sensed he had a problem: how to get back down those steps to his parents!

The child called for his father to come up and get him, but the father stood still and beckoned for the child to come down alone. The little adventurer was full of fear and began to act defiantly; he stamped his feet and protested. The father kept his peace and held his place. Finally the child tired of protesting. He cautiously and cryingly descended the stairs, moving slowly at first, and all of the adults standing below were quite anxious for him. They all knew that a fall could be damaging and perhaps fatal. When he at last reached the bottom step, the child rushed confidently into the arms of his waiting father, who hugged him warmly, and the parents and child walked on down the street with the family now at ease again.[1]

Why did that father allow such risk in dealing with his little child? He allowed it for the same reason that God lets us experience stress: it is all important to our process as maturing persons.

That father risked his child's action in the spirit of love for him. So does God when dealing with us. God does not spare us the stress of risks and ventures that goad and develop us on our human journey.

Life does have its hard spots. It is filled with peril. Life can often seem like a giant system of trial, with no apparent reason or purpose. But faith sees more than what our feelings tell us. There is a level in godliness that life cannot readily disturb. And the awareness that we are in process—under God's wise guidance—can make the strain we feel along the journey more easily handled.

Something deep within us all tells us that stress does not have to destroy us. Something deep within us tells us that God can deliver us from the deadliest perils—not always by taking us around them but sometimes through them. Paul understood this and confessed, "He delivered us from so deadly a peril, and he will deliver us; on him we have set our hope that he will deliver us again."

[1]See Douglas V. Steere, *On Beginning from Within* (New York: Harper and Brothers, 1943), esp. pp. 65-66.